The Good, the Bad and the Ugly
The Story of 45 Mixed Up No. 1 Songs

Richard Taylor

ISBN: 978-1-916732-38-4

Copyright 2024

All rights reserved. No part of this publication may be reproduced, stored in a retrieval system, or transmitted in any form or by any means, electronic, mechanical, photocopy, recording or otherwise, without prior written consent of the copyright owner. Nor can it be circulated in any form of binding or cover other than that in which it is published and without similar condition including this condition being imposed on a subsequent purchaser. The right of Richard Taylor to be identified as the author of this work has been asserted in accordance with the Copyright Designs and Patents Act 1988. A copy of this book is deposited with the British Library.

Published by:

i2i
PUBLISHING

www.i2ipublishing.co.uk
i2i Publishing, Manchester.

Contents

Acknowledgements v
Intro – A Book Start vii
The Photographs xvii
Chapter 1 – I Want to Hold Your Hand – The Beatles 1
Chapter 2 – (I Can't Get No) Satisfaction –
             The Rolling Stones 5
Chapter 3 – Good Vibrations – The Beach Boys 9
Chapter 4 – Release Me – Engelbert Humperdinck 13
Chapter 5 – The Good, the Bad and the Ugly –
             Hugo Montenegro 17
Chapter 6 – Je T'aime… Moi Non Plus –
             Jane Birkin and Serge Gainsbourg 21
Chapter 7 – Back Home – England World Cup Squad 25
Chapter 8 – Grandad – Clive Dunn 29
Chapter 9 – Telegram Sam – T. Rex 33
Chapter 10 – Cum On Feel the Noize – Slade 39
Chapter 11 – Billy Don't Be a Hero – Paper Lace 43
Chapter 12 – Bohemian Rhapsody – Queen 47
Chapter 13 – The Combine Harvester (Brand New Key) –
              The Wurzels 53
Chapter 14 – Knowing Me, Knowing You – ABBA 57
Chapter 15 – Wuthering Heights – Kate Bush 63
Chapter 16 – Video Killed the Radio Star – Buggles 67
Chapter 17 – There's No One Quite Like Grandma –
              St. Winifred's School Choir 71
Chapter 18 – Tainted Love – Soft Cell 77
Chapter 19 – Come On Eileen – Dexys Midnight Runners .. 81
Chapter 20 – Billie Jean – Michael Jackson 85
Chapter 21 – Do They Know It's Christmas? Band Aid 91
Chapter 22 – 19 – Paul Hardcastle 97

Chapter 23	– The Chicken Song – Spitting Image	101
Chapter 24	– It's a Sin – Pet Shop Boys	105
Chapter 25	– He Ain't Heavy, He's My Brother – The Hollies	109
Chapter 26	– Ride on Time – Black Box	113
Chapter 27	– Vogue – Madonna	117
Chapter 28	– (Everything I Do), I Do It for You – Bryan Adams	121
Chapter 29	– Deeply Dippy – Right Said Fred	125
Chapter 30	– Mr Blobby – Mr Blobby	129
Chapter 31	– Love Is All Around – Wet Wet Wet	133
Chapter 32	– Some Might Say – Oasis	137
Chapter 33	– Wannabe – Spice Girls	141
Chapter 34	– Candle in the Wind '97 – Elton John	145
Chapter 35	– Millennium – Robbie Williams	151
Chapter 36	– Livin' la Vida Loca – Ricky Martin	155
Chapter 37	– Spinning Around – Kylie Minogue	159
Chapter 38	– Mambo No. 5 – Bob the Builder	163
Chapter 39	– A Little Less Conversation – Elvis vs JXL	167
Chapter 40	– Crazy in Love – Beyoncé	171
Chapter 41	– Call on Me – Eric Prydz	175
Chapter 42	– (Is This the Way to) Amarillo – Tony Christie with Peter Kay	181
Chapter 43	– Hips Don't Lie – Shakira with Wyclef Jean	185
Chapter 44	– 1979: Another Brick in the Wall – Pink Floyd	189
Chapter 45	– 1967: A Whiter Shade of Pale – Procol Harum	193
A Book End	– Outro	197
Bibliography		203

Acknowledgements

I would like to say thanks to my long-suffering wife Linda, who is married to a strange man who thinks he can write a book. She is a great source of encouragement and has done a great job of initial proofreading, where she is able to dot my 't's, cross my 'i's and vice versa.

I would like to thank everybody at i2i Publishing including Lionel Ross, the top man and for being a top man, Richard A. Smith for brilliant proofreading and editing, Jess Gibbard for the procurement of wonderful photographs and Dino Caruana for the fabulous cover design.

Finally, I must thank all of the fantastic 45 artists, yes even you Mr Blobby, for producing the single soundtrack of my life!

Intro: A Book Start

I have always been fascinated by the pop single charts, certainly way back when the weekly ritual of checking to see if your favourites had got to No. 1 was so important. What made a No. 1 single, who bought the 45s and why were some No. 1s obviously great records, while others were… er, to put it bluntly, a bit dubious? Not mentioning names at this stage for dubiosity, though in a recent email from Mr Blobby he did ask me to find out just why he got to No. 1 in 1993. He was as perplexed as the rest of us. First, a bit of history.

The pop charts for singles were started in 1952 by Percy Dickins of the New Musical Express (NME). He phoned 20 record stores for their sales of 45 vinyl singles on a weekly basis and used that sample to make up a chart based on sales. Before this there was a singles chart based on the sale of sheet music. The first No. 1 based on this sample was Al Martino "Here Is My Heart". The sales figures for singles continued to be collected in a similar way through retailers phoning or writing in sales, till automated barcode sales were relayed through the tills from 1994. Up until 1969 every music paper, The NME, Melody Maker, Record Mirror, and Disc had their own separate charts. During this time, the BBC used an aggregate average from the music papers for its own unique chart. However, post-1969 the chart became standardised for all, when the sales were collected by the British Market Research Bureau, which then took samples from 250 shops. Downloads were finally added to the chart in 2005.

A single is a release of a song(s) that is shorter than the whole LP, traditionally having the main song on the A side and the subsidiary song on the B side. In 1949 the first 7 inch 45 revolutions per minute (rpm) single was released. By 1964 this 45 rpm 7 inch was standard for all singles. Therefore 45 songs has to be a suitable number of singles to examine and analyse for this book over the 42 years of Top of the Pops between 1964 and 2006 (more on this later). Books of this ilk tend to pick 100 or 50 as suitable round numbers such as "A History of the World in 100 Objects", etc, but for an examination of No. 1 singles why not do 45 of them? As indicated earlier, that was the rpm of a single 45 on a gramophone turntable. Luckily, I am not doing a classical book, or it might be 78 magnificent symphonies to analyse. My father was a classical obsessive and had 78 rpm 12-inch vinyl (about 4 to a symphony) records stored all over the house in multiple cases. Now, of course, you can get it all on your phone or memory stick, and most vinyl bought by old timers is buried in the loft or spare bedroom. The peak year for the sale of vinyl singles globally was 1974 with 200 million sold. Vinyl began to disappear in the '80s, to be replaced by tape singles, followed by CD singles and then towards the end of our time period in 2006, was augmented by downloads and streaming.

So, by the late 50s and early '60s, young people, mainly teenagers, would wait avidly for the new charts to come out, to see if their favourite song was going to be No. 1. Pre-Top of the Pops (TOTP), which we will come to soon, the best way was to listen to the BBC radio Light Programme and in particular to Pick of the Pops (POTP). It started in 1955, then transferring to the new Radio 1 in 1967 and mainly ran on a late Sunday afternoon. The best-known presenter here taking over in 1962 was Alan "pop pickers" Freeman. As a prepubescent, I just used to love listening to the programme, where Alan was the consummate presenter for a chart run down. "Not half" and "pop pickers" were some of his catchphrases, as he built up to playing the No. 1 at the end of the show. It was so exciting for an under 10-year-old, reminding me with my young sporting brain, of a race commentary. I was not that bothered about the music, but I just loved Alan's manic vocal delivery. He stayed for 39 years till 2000, being replaced by Dale Winton till 2010 and therefore passing over the final year of 2006 for the No. 1s in this book. For people older than me, now in their seventies and eighties, who as youngsters rolled Beethoven over and got into pop, then the POTP chart was the only way to experience the musical countdown to No. 1. For many before TOTP, this was a weekly episodic event that was not to be missed. There was no satellite TV, no mobile phones, no internet, no social media, not even pirate radio out in the North Sea, which did not come alive till 1964. How did people cope with no electronic devices? Well, they did and some of us are around now to prove it with a little bit of sanity/insanity intact. Don't get me wrong; with all the information systems and data today, daily life is infinitely better. Those weren't the days!

TOTP started on the 1st of January 1964. There was a further need commercially to tap into teenagers, who as a species were relatively new, but had some "never had it so good" monetary spending power, or at least their better off parents did. Promoting the charts and pop music was good for business. Over the next 42 years it would prove to be a lot of fun too. This first TOTP programme featured Dusty Springfield "I Only Want to Be with You", the Rolling Stones "I Wanna Be Your Man" (written by Lennon and McCartney), the Dave Clark 5 with "Glad All Over", "Stay" from the Hollies, the Swinging Blue Jeans with "Hippy Hippy Shake" and finally at No. 1, the Beatles singing "I Want to Hold Your Hand". Unfortunately, there is no archive film of this first ever TOTP. I would like to say as a snotty 8-year-old that I watched it, but no, I didn't. I am not even sure we had a TV by then, we certainly did not have a car, luckily, we (just about) had an indoor toilet. I had a vague interest in pop music and persuaded my dad to buy me a couple of 7 inch 45 singles "She Loves You" which preceded "I Want to Hold Your Hand" at No. 1 and the "Twist and Shout" extended play (EP) single which had 2 songs on each side ("Twist and Shout", "A Taste of Honey", flipped over to "Do You Want To Know a Secret" and "There's a Place") All those songs of course were by the Fab Four Beatles. To do this for the EP, the songs were compressed from an ordinary two song single, which meant they were a lot quieter, which was a shame because "Twist and Shout" was meant to be played loud. However, soon like everyone else of my young generation I became a TOTP addict.

By late 1964 TOTP had moved to its traditional spot on a Thursday at 7.35pm and by 1970 was attracting 15 million viewers weekly. It was a programme that was talked about at school, in the workplace and had iconic status across the nation. Who was No. 1 was important for millions of people. There were eventually 2,272 episodes of TOTP. There were hundreds of singers, bands, oddities and assorted lunatics who appeared over the years, sometimes on multiple occasions. Status Quo hold the record for the most appearances, being 87, starting with "Pictures of Matchstick Men" from 1968 to "The Party Ain't Over Yet" from 2005.

However, things change, as they always do. By the noughties people could access numerous sources for pop music and pop music chart information. MTV and other satellite TV music channels, the internet with YouTube, it was all there then as it is in 2024, perhaps now with just faster streaming speeds. TOTP was becoming old school and old hat. By 2005 only 3 million a week were now watching, and the show was on BBC2 on a Sunday night, but even this had then dramatically halved to 1.5 million in 2006. So, the Beeb decided to cut their losses and closed it down with the last show being on 30th July 2006. The final acts were the Rolling Stones who opened the show with appropriately "The Last Time" followed by the Spice Girls, David Bowie, Wham, Madonna, Beyoncé, Gnarls Barkley, the Jackson Five, Sonny and Cher and Robbie Williams. All was finished off with the No. 1 on the 30th of June by Shakira with Wyclef Jean singing "Hips Don't Lie". (Disgraced) Jimmy Savile, who had also presented the first edition, then literally turned out the lights in the studio and that was that after 42 years.

42 years of hits and No. 1s is very much a suitable time range for this book, as this is the time range of TOTP. All the No.

1s in the book were featured on TOTP during the 42 years. It is not to say there have not been No. 1s before 1964 and after 2006, but I had to draw a chronological line somewhere. If I did a book from 1952 to now, I could be writing forever without so much as a toilet or meal break and that would never do. Also, the book would be zillions of words long and never be finished before bedtime. Anyway, add in two bonus No. 1 song tracks completely free of charge and you have 45 in total, which just happens to be the revolutions per minute (rpm) on a turntable of a vinyl 7-inch naturally named 45 single. It could be said to be the Golden Age of the classic pop single, at least for most of these years from 1964 to 2006. But what No. 1 could I pick from each year? To be interesting, I would have to make the singles as differently mixed as possible. It may include serious songs, love songs, joke songs, children's songs and awfully (good/bad) songs that still got to No. 1. You could say I would have to pick singles that were "good, bad and ugly" but all got to be a No. 1 in each year from 1964 to 2006.

A good song is one that was an all-time classic, has emotional resonance with millions and is stuck in the collective consciousness of the nation. "Hey Jude" by the Beatles or "Dancing Queen" by ABBA are examples. A good pop single should have a catchy melody, "everyperson" lyrics easily understood; the chorus should be unforgettable, foot-tappable and sing-along. It needs to be well aurally presented, be well produced and be 3 to 3:30 minutes long. It should resonate emotionally with the listener and tap into their personal experiences if possible. It needs to be a subjective, relatable experience. Is it any wonder that love songs are very popular for singles? These of course are massive generalisations. "The Good, the Bad and the Ugly" (see Chapter 5) as an instrumental should never have got to No. 1 with no lyrics but it did, as did "Albatross", a very uncommercial sounding instrumental from Fleetwood Mac in 1969. Records with dance grooves (not vinyl grooves), in a disco, dance format, where chorus and verse become blurred, associated with few lyrics can also do well. Witness and listen to "Call on Me" by Eric Prydz for this type of No. 1 from 2005. Mind you, the video for this song might just have helped (see Chapter 41 for more). Which leaves the mad bad ugly sad ones that still got to No. 1! No names at the moment.

A bad song in the context of this weighty tome may be considered to be such a bad song that it is awful. So awfully bad in fact that it becomes memorable, and it may become both ironically iconic or vice versa. An ugly song is one of those "How the **** did that song ever get to No. 1?" moments because it is so weird, wacky and bizarre that you wonder why anyone bought it in the first place. Some songs can be both bad and ugly or even take on all three qualities in the first verse. At this stage I am not at further liberty to reveal a bad or an ugly song or any bad, ugly songs, due to the threat of legal action or physical violence for negative comments. I have just reread Mr Blobby's email from the first paragraph and he does say any negative comment about his self-named No. 1 (1993) will result in myself being severely squashed and squished. Meanwhile, a further communication from Bob the Builder has threatened to brick me up behind a wall, if I say anything bad about him and his No. 1 "Mambo No. 5" from 2001. I can't tell you what the Wurzels (1996) will do to me with their combine harvester if I criticise their Numero Uno. So, I have to take a bit of care!

The bonus tracks, to make up the 45, are additional No. 1 songs from 1979, and 1967. All the songs are iconic in different ways and have something to say about themselves in a "good, bad or ugly" way. Meanwhile what, where and when was "The Good, the Bad and the Ugly?" Well, I digress…

The Film "The Good, the Bad and the Ugly" was a 1966 Spaghetti Western film by Sergio Leonie in involving a three-way contest (the wrestling analogy is deliberate) between "good" Clint Eastwood, "bad" Lee Van Cleef and "ugly" Eli Wallach to see who can find some stray discarded gold first. Eli

Wallach is certainly ugly (but very funny as a character in the film). Lee Van Cleef's bad character had never heard of morals, ethics or just niceness, not being the sort of chap you would want as a neighbour, while Clint (supposedly good) was not actually much better. However, the final three-way shootout is very tense, dramatic and a great watch. It also produced a fantastic soundtrack, "The Good, the Bad and the Ugly" by Ennio Morricone. The main theme from the soundtrack was covered by Hugo Montenegro, which just happened to be released as "The Good, the Bad and the Ugly", a No. 1 instrumental single in 1968 (see Chapter 4). It is also, I hope, a rather good title for this book to represent the interesting range of mixed-up No. 1 songs, which I have chosen.

So, No. 1 singles can be good, bad or ugly. As you go through the chapter headings and the book, it is clearly obvious at a glance that some of the selected No. 1s are better than others. Yet of course they all go to No. 1. Why? This book will hopefully try to answer that. Just how can the Beatles and St. Winifred's School Choir be in the same chart and have No. 1 singles? It's still a mystery… for now.

With the songs, I have tried to pick a real mixture of "good, bad and ugly". It is not meant to be the best song of the year that everybody would vote for, if allowed. It is personal subjective choice to make the book hopefully more interesting and entertaining! Anyway, beauty is in the ear of the beholder, and you might quite rightly have your own views. What is a good single for me might be a bad or ugly one for you and vice versa. Sometimes where a song is "having a laugh" it turns it round, making it good, even though on first hearing we may not like it. To be serious, humour in the form of gentle irony is really important in popular chart music. Even "low level it's just the charts" culture can be enhanced by humour that has an accessible common touch that we can all relate to. Gosh, I am beginning to sound a bit too serious.

For each song in the book, I will try my best to define what made it so collectively popular in the eyes of the public. This is definitely one of the great fun challenges for me while writing this book and one of the great questions of our time that is begging to be answered (really? … yep definitely!). I will try to answer this head on with intelligence, academic rigour and a serious face, with just a hint of slight humour to spice up the text.

Just looking at my list lyrically, love and romance issues do predominate, probably followed by having a good time and partying words. Maybe next are lyrics about youthful rebellion, others are blatantly about sex and sexual innuendo (well one is). Finally, there a few weird and wacky comedy songs, where it is probably best to be about three years old or blind drunk when you listen to them. I am not always brilliant with lyrics. Luckily, most No. 1s are easy to follow. The two No. 1 songs with "We skipped the light fandango" or "can you do the fandango" lyrics (can you guess which ones?) might be a bit tricky. All will be lyrically and wordily revealed in the chapters.

I will also look at the musicality of said song and track. Guitars, drums, synthesisers, tambourines and samples will all get a mention. From the Bohemian Rhapsody video (1975) onwards, the music video which became a massive selling point in some cases, being better known than the song, will also be looked at.

There are a few songs in the list that are so profoundly moving, and emotionally resonating that they will be played and talked about in a hundred years' time on the Moon, Mars and the Earth. These are the classics everybody would more or less agree with. This is where I have to apologise profusely for missing out those other classic fantastic songs not mentioned. I had to make a choice though and take a sample. If you compiled your own list for these years, what would you choose? What type of songs would they be if you wanted a balance of "good, bad and ugly"? My rule for the book is that they had to be No.

1s. Three absolutely famous songs for example that only got to No. 2 were "Penny Lane/Strawberry Fields" by the Beatles in 1967, the notoriously banned "God Save the Queen" by the Sex Pistols in 1976, while "Wonderwall" from Oasis in 1995 just missed the top spot too. It is a shame I cannot include these songs.

A note on the "Sales UK" figures included for every single at the top of the chapter. They were quite tricky to pin down, in that some of the figures were just for the period the singles were No. 1 or in the charts that year, while some were the figures of sales in a lifetime up to 2024, including downloads and streaming. Therefore, the figures are a little nebulous but will be broadly accurate. I would estimate a low selling No. 1 would need a minimum of 200,000 copies and I have used this figure as a best guess for a few of the singles that I could not find any sales figures for. This is indicated by "200,000 approx." for the "Sales UK" for those songs. On some occasions famous No. 2s, as indicated in the previous paragraph, would ordinarily have sold more than enough to get to the top unless the actual No. 1 had sold zillions more. This was the case with our favourite No. 2 "Penny Lane/Strawberry Fields" by the Beatles which sold 500,000 in 1967, only then to lose out to million seller "Release Me" by Engelbert Humperdinck, which hogged the top spot. This is one of life's great mysteries, as to why Engelbert surpassed the Fab Four, which I will try to explain in Chapter 4. If, as rumoured in the next paragraph, I might do a chart rundown of my selected 45 45s, it will be interesting to compare my choices with the actual sales figures.

In the A Book End: Outro chapter, if the money has not run out, I might just do some lists. All books seem to have lists now, again all subjectively to be chosen as "best to worst" or the other way round. I have an idea not many of you though would disagree too much with my top 10 choices, or perhaps my No. 45. In between is open to much debate and argument. If any of you wish to argue with me personally at this stage, can I point out I will have already left the building and then subsequently will be out to lunch that day. After that I will be working on the rumoured next book.

Time to start the rest of this book. Wish me luck!

The Photographs

Each chapter has a photograph, which pictorially represents that song. Some of the photographs are obvious and not too clever and some are weirdly obtuse and are far too clever for their own good, while the silent majority meet nicely in the middle. They are there to entertain, be a talking point and for you dear reader, to be ever so slightly perplexed and have a think about what they mean and how they are relevant to the song.

The photos may be based on the song title and/or the song lyrics, as well as the artist name. They may be linked to the back, present or front story of the said song as expressed in the text of the chapter. The challenge is there for you to work them out, but before you ask for a refund, here are some clues for 7 of the songs.

In Chapter 2 for "(I Can't Get No) Satisfaction" by the Rolling Stones: the first line, first verse is "When I'm drivin' in my car". I would imagine Mick Jagger driving his E Type Jag "And a man comes on the radio" (second line, first verse).

In Chapter 8 for "Grandad" by Clive Dunn: Clive in his TOTP appearances sat in a rocking chair.

In Chapter 9 for "Telegram Sam" by T. Rex: main man Marc Bolan had corkscrew hair, and this is referenced in the lyric "I ain't no square with my corkscrew hair".

In Chapter 18 for Tainted Love by Soft Cell: a breakup song so... a bit of a "too clever by half" photo here. The author blames the editor and vice versa.

In Chapter 27 for Vogue by Madonna: a black and white song video was made for "Vogue", hence the appropriate black and white photo.

In Chapter 33 for Wannabe by the Spice Girls: the song video was made in the Midland Grand Hotel, at St Pancras, London, which is pictured.

Chapter 43 for Hips Don't Lie by Shakira: the author compares "I Want to Hold Your Hand" from 1964 by the Beatles to "Hips Don't Lie" by Shakira in 2006, in the chapter text, hence the "Hands on Hips" photo.

That is your starter for 7. Good luck and much fun with the rest!

xx

Chapter 1

I Want to Hold Your Hand: The Beatles

Released 29 November 1963
No. 1 for 5 weeks
12 December '63 to 9 January '64
Sales UK: 1.8m

It is only fitting that the song that starts this book is by the Beatles, you may just have heard of them and they need little introduction. Most people have some inkling of their back-story prior to 1964 and what happened afterwards up to the 1970 split. By this stage in '64 Beatlemania had broken out and they could not go out in public without being mobbed. They still wore their suits, had their Beatle mops and said all the right zany things in press conferences. If we do forget any of this, Paul and Ringo are still around to prod us and remind us of these events. If they forget anything, there are zillions of Beatle books and Fab Four websites around to remind them. It is nearly an absolute fact that according to most charts that matter and the one I am using, "I Want to Hold Your Hand" was their 3rd No. 1 single after "From Me to You" and "She Loves You" (Some other charts do have "Please Please Me" getting to No. 1 too).

I had been introduced to the Beatles as a fresh faced 8-year-old with "She Loves You", which I persuaded my dad to take me out to buy, along with the "Twist and Shout" extended play (EP) single. Even my classical loving Dad appreciated the five-part harmony in the last few seconds of "She Loves You" and told me that while they were not Bach or Beethoven, they were nice boys and could do well. I was allowed to play it at low–medium volume on our monstrously massive radiogram just once a day along with the "Twist and Shout", routinely bookended by my dad's Beethoven symphonies out on 78. It was very much a case of roll over Beatles rather than vice versa in our household. When "I Want to Hold Your Hand" came out, I liked the song but had run out of pocket money, so it was back to listening on the BBC radio Light Programme to Pick of the Pops on a Sunday, hoping it might just crop up as No. 1. It did in mid-December '63.

The song was written by John and Paul eyeball to eyeball on acoustic guitars and then translated into a full band production, with the addition of George and Ringo. All four Beatles were on percussive addition in the form of handclaps. Both writers have mysteriously talked about a magic chord that started the song off, but whatever it was and wherever it is, it did lend the song an exuberance and uplifting warmth in the wonderful music.

With the singing, John takes the lead, Paul sings the higher harmony, which is especially strident on the "Hands" and "Hide" lyrical moments where the vocals lift up just for the one word. The vocals are very clear, and it is but a simple love song. Every word is clearly enunciated and easy to follow. That is unless you are Bob Dylan. He thought he heard "I get high" instead of "I can't hide" thinking the Fab Four were already turned on to the stoned delights of Cannabis. When Bob eventually met the Beatles in August 1964 he was eventually reappraised of the correct lyric. Naturally as a thank you, he rolled our heroes a monster spliff, so they could mishear too. Beatle mythology has it that Bob first turned the lads on to love, peace and dope.

Bizarrely, along with "She Loves You", the Beatles recorded a German version for the German speaking market of "I Want to Hold Your Hand" that sounded like this: "Komm Gib Mir Deine Hand" which literally means "Come, Give Me Your Hand". I wonder what Bob The Dylan misheard in that one?

It was eventually released as a single at the end of November '63, being 2:24 minutes long and backed on the B side by "This Boy". It first got to No. 1 on the 12th of December replacing "She Loves You". It was still No. 1 at the start of '64.

The Fab Four reigned supreme and were omnipresent across the nation.

The first Top of the Pops was on the 1st of January 1964 at 6.35 pm. The Beatles closed the show with a pre-recorded version of the song. The BBC tape of this does not exist anymore. The only live TOTP studio recording of the Quality Quartet to be saved was that of "Paperback Writer" from 1966, available on all good social media outlets. We have to wait until the Ed Sullivan Show on the 2nd of September 1964 to have any film of the Beatles doing "Hand" live. Interestingly, back on the same TOTP, a little known R'n'B combo from London, the Rolling Stones, were on doing "I Wanna Be Your Man" another giveaway Lennon and McCartney number, originally sung by Ringo on the With the Beatles album. However, things were to change dramatically for the Stones by 1965! (see next chapter).

It was the Beatles' first American hit, earlier songs then being hits retrospectively. It eventually sold 12m copies worldwide. In 2004 Rolling Stone magazine ranked it the 16th greatest song of all time and in 2010 the same magazine ranked it the second greatest Fab Four song of all time after "A Day in the Life". It is the 18th biggest-selling single of all time in the UK. We can quietly conclude that this little ditty has done quite well for itself.

For me, it is a middle to highish Beatle song although I recognise its inherent greatness. Of the early classics, "She Loves You" remains my favourite. Of all their output my overall favourite would perhaps be "A Day in the Life", followed by sing-along "Hey Jude". However, it definitely goes up in my estimation as Bob Dylan misheard the lyrics, which I always have found amusing. This is a great first song to start the book and perhaps likely to be in my top 10 of the 45 songs I have chosen.

Chapter 2

(I Can't Get No) Satisfaction: The Rolling Stones

Released 4 June 1965
No. 1 for 2 weeks
9 September to 16 September '65
Sales UK: 600,000

"(I Can't Get No) Satisfaction", to give it the full title is still a song I can listen to today for pleasure. I have never tired of it; neither have the Stones or their audiences. It has become the 5th most live played Stones song with 973 performances, after "Jumping Jack Flash" (1,196), "Brown Sugar" (1,137 now retired because of controversial lyrics), "Honky Tonk Woman" (1,137), and "Tumbling Dice" (1,122), (data from 24/1/24). In other words, it is an absolutely classic pop rock song that millions know and love to this day. They just don't get any bigger or better known than this until… perhaps next year's No. 1?

It all starts with a Keith Richards riff that he claims came to him in his sleep. It goes "de-der, de-de-der, de-de-de-de-de" and of course comes over far better in sound than a scribe attempting to write it in "der der" language. When Keith awoke, he recorded the riff on acoustic guitar, and fell asleep leaving the tape on recording his snores. Now if these had been left on the final version just think how much bigger the song would have been (K. R. on snoring guitar!). As is his wont, Mick then wrote the lyrics. To thicken and sustain the famous riff, a guitar add-on called a fuzz box was used, which was supposed to sound like saxophones. Whatever it was, it did the trick and became the song's main musical motif.

Lyrically it was all rebellious stuff where the younger generation, well Mick anyway, can find no satisfaction with blatant commercialism. On the other hand, the line about "girl reaction" indicated a certain sexual frustration inherent, quite shocking for 1965. So the song could have two meanings, quite advanced ironic lyrics for 1965. As the years went by, I don't suppose Mick in particular objected to commercialism and capitalism that sold Stones records. He also seemed to do well with women as well, but apparently not as well as quiet moody bass player Bill Wyman. All these facts and myths out there about sex, drugs and rock'n'roll re the Stones are available in all good books, magazines, websites and gossip columns.

Needless to say, poll after poll has ranked the song in the top this or that over the years. Maybe the best accolade is that in a 2004 poll, Rolling Stone ranked it the 2nd best greatest song of all time, just behind "Like a Rolling Stone" by Bob Dylan. By 2021 it had slipped down the Rolling Stones Chart to No 31. Shame! However, it remains universally loved and popular. "Satisfaction" (and rock'n'roll) can never die. It is out there like Beethoven, the Beatles and Mr Blobby (really?) as a part of our collective musical experience forever.

There are some notable cover versions. One is by Otis Redding, where saxophones play the famous riff in a rhythm and blues soul style, while another famous non-rocker pop star, Britney Spears did a funk dance version. Who would have thought? It's not bad, but the repeated every 4th beat snare drum sounds like it was played on a biscuit tin. Alternatively, wonderful, weird and wacky early '80s new wave band Devo do an amazing version. Could be good or could be bad? Er… you decide, check it out; music is always in the ear of the beholder.

As I listen to the original song now, just why is it so good? Well, the riff of course, but how about the driving incessant drumming from the great Charlie Watts, subtlety augmented by an incessantly driving tambourine. Mick's pitch raising singing voice at the end is a vocal masterstroke for a great exciting ending. Of the original players on the single, Bill Wyman, on bass, is in his mid '80s and happily retired. Brian Jones who played guitars, keyboards and harmonica, passed away in dubious circumstances in 1969. The late, wonderful Charlie Watts played the magnificent drums on the track, leaving Mick Jagger and Keith Richards to sing and play guitar. Amazingly, Mick at 80 looks older in the face perhaps but has the body of a 20-year-old and can still sing falsetto. How does he do it? Keith never looked young to start with, but he can still play and caress a guitar with the best of them in his 80th year. I have this feeling all is well in the world while the Rolling Stones are still out, playing "Satisfaction" for their encore somewhere in a concert hall. Long may that continue! A top 5 song for my outro list… definitely maybe?

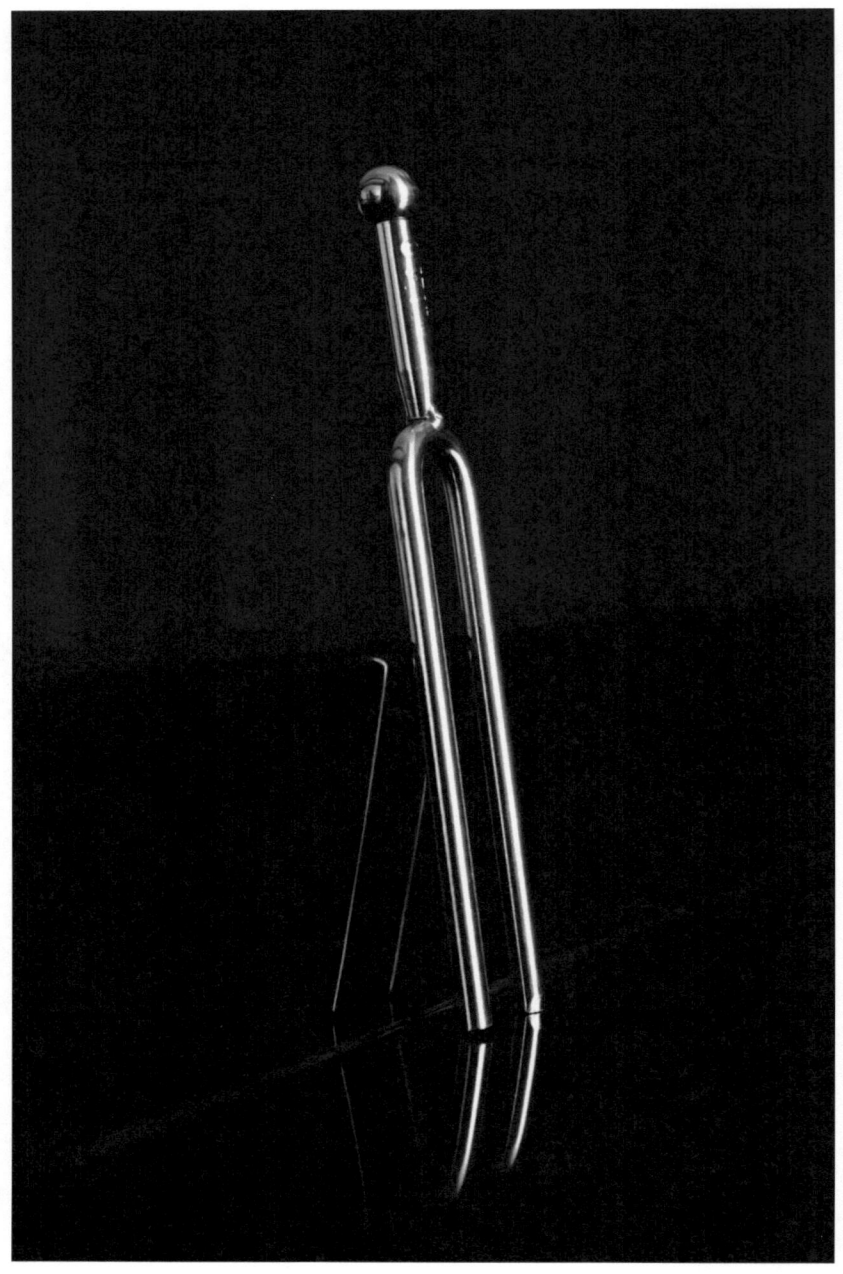

Chapter 3

Good Vibrations: The Beach Boys

Released 10 October 1966
No. 1 for 2 weeks
17 November to 24 November '66
Sales UK: 600,000

This is quite simply one of the best songs of all time in many people's ears, including mine. Another track I will play for fun 58 years later. There have probably been more books, magazines, internet websites and general commentary on this particular song than any other in history. Yet it could be argued it is not even the Beach Boys' greatest song, some might say "God Only Knows" is better. That song however, only got to No. 2 though in July 1966. It was in that year that both these songs came out and you might argue that the Beach Boys, and writer Brian Wilson in particular, were going through a purple patch. The catalyst for this immense bout of creativity was the Beatles.

Amazingly, the song was recorded in stages and bits between Feb '66 and Sep '66 and uses the six Beach Boys, but then additionally used 23 session musicians and three engineers. And it only lasted 3:35 minutes! The cost was reputedly up to 100,000 dollars to make. The recording history is well-documented elsewhere and everywhere, so a quick summary only is in order here or we might not get home in time for Christmas.

The song was recorded in fragments at different times with different people. Only Brian Wilson could perhaps see the total picture in his mind through this lengthy process. There were 90 hours of tape recorded, so a little editing had to be done for just 3:35 minutes! The most unusual instrument used was the theremin. This was able to give the weird science fiction warbling ghost sounds heard intermittently throughout the instrumental track, especially at the end. It was a device invented in 1928 by Leon Theremin. It involved waving hands about between two antennas, thus breaking up an electromagnetic field to produce up and down strange wobbly sounds. The electro theremin invented in the 1950s by a Paul Tanner, a trombone player, made the sound easier to manipulate. It was this that was used on "Good Vibrations". The other major use of a theremin in popular music was in the middle freak out section of "Whole Lotta Love" by Led Zeppelin in 1969.

Brian Wilson coined the "Good Vibrations" title. As a child, his mum had told him that dogs could pick up bad cosmic vibrations from people. Therefore, it is as well to have "good vibrations" as a definite help as a dog owner and to resonate well with other people, who subliminally respond to a person's positive or negative vibrations. Could just be hippy dippy stuff, dogs are more likely to respond to your bad BO perhaps? "Good Smelling" as a title would just not have cut the mustard like "Good Vibrations".

The actual lyrics were written by singer Mike Love and were very much boy fancies girl lyrics. One line was "I'm pickin' up good vibrations, She's giving me excitations". I can only presume if I had used this line: "Hello, you are giving me excitations" with a girl as a teenager then I might have made up for my acne, BO and appalling dress sense. Lead vocals were shared between Mike, Brian and Carl Wilson.

For the instrumental track there are six different musical motifs, thus it was described by Beach Boys publicist Derek Taylor as a "pocket symphony" and paved a way for future mini symphonic epics like "Bohemian Rhapsody", which also cost a small fortune and took aeons to record (see Chapter 12).

In 1966 Brian Wilson as writer, arranger and creator was at his zenith, but then he had been spurred on by the epic pop sensibilities of the Beatles. The timeline goes like this. Brian was blown away by Rubber Soul, the Fab Four 1965 album (the one with "Yesterday" on). In turn, the Beatles were blown more away by the Pet Sounds album put out by the Beach Boys in 1965. That led to Brian's two single masterpieces "God Only Knows" then "Good Vibrations". The Beatles could only offer "Penny Lane/Strawberry Fields" in return, not a bad little reply! Revolver, the Beatles album from 1966, past Brian by but not Sergeant Pepper from 1967. This included the track "She's Leaving Home" which Brian became obsessed by, and he was spurred on to try and top it. He was going to respond with an even better album called Smile, which was to include "Good Vibrations" as its first track… and then it stopped, and the album never came out in 1967! A version "Brian Wilson presents Smile" came out in 2004. By Mid '67 poor young Brian succumbed to drug and mental health problems well documented in Beach Boys mythology. But for a year in 1966 Brian Wilson and the Beach Boys shone brighter than the sun!

"Good Vibrations" was showered with praise and excitations about its glory. It was No. 6 in the greatest songs of all time in the 500 hundred greatest Rolling Stone magazine list, up until the early noughties, and then fell to 53 in the 2021 edition. The 21st century must have produced some fantastic songs to knock our first three No. 1s in the book through '64, '65 and '66, down the Rolling Stone list?

I am, to put it mildly, rather fond of Good Vibrations. Is it the greatest song on my list? I am not sure, but it could finish in the top 1, or in the top10? You will have to wait for the Book End: Outro to find out, though you could sneak a look now, I suppose. I won't tell anyone!

Chapter 4

Release Me: Engelbert Humperdinck

Released 26 January 1967
No. 1 for 6 weeks
28 February to 11 April '67
Sales UK: 1.38m

1967 was the year of the Beatles and Sergeant Pepper. The talk on the streets was of the counterculture, revolution and "be sure to wear some flowers in your hair". Yet the biggest selling single of the year was by a then little-known ballad crooner called Arnold George Dorsey. Meanwhile, the original Engelbert Humperdinck was a German classical composer best known for writing Hansel and Gretel as an opera. He died in 1921, which is just as well as Mr A. G. Dorsey took his name as a quirky promotional tool in 1965. What a strange thing to do? But it certainly worked. Not only did Arnold/Engelbert sell lots of records in his glory year of 1967, but he also then became very much a sex symbol, attracting hordes of female admirers called "Humperdinckers", who stuck with him over the years and he eventually went on to have a substantial musical career. Move over Tom Jones, probably his biggest rival in terms of style, looks and songs at that time.

He had two monster hits in '67, "Release Me" followed by "The Last Waltz", both million sellers being 1.38m and 1.17m respectively. I personally prefer "The Last Waltz" with its sad lyrics about the last waltz at the dance with the woman who falls out of love with Engelbert (was that possible?). It has very clear, easily understood lyrics and is very much a smooth classic, not half bad in my opinion.

As for "Release Me", that is something else. Personally, it does not do anything for me, and it is one of those "How did this get to No. 1?" moments. It was written by Eddie Miller,

Robert Yount and Dub Williams Miller way back in 1949. There were several disputes about authorship over the years, not surprising when there was so much money to be had in 1967. There were single versions here and there over the years, not really doing too much, until Engelbert appropriated it in early 1967. It got to No. 1 on the 28$^{th\ of}$ February, staying there for six weeks.

Lyrically it says I don't love you anymore, you need to let me go, release me from my love contract with you. Oh dear, had they seen a marriage councillor? In fact, apart from a few (mainly unsuccessful) paternity suits, as you do, if you have "Humperdinckers" female fans following you everywhere, Engelbert was happily married to Patricia from 1964 till her passing in 2021. Musically the track is slow and slower, music to nod off to. Engelbert's deep vibrato begging vocals were retro even for 1967. As I continue to write this chapter at this point, I continue to be bemused as to why this song got to No. 1. Yet… it did!

Whatever you or I may think of it, the song was a massive seller. Why? is the big question. Despite the air of change, with hippydom, drug taking and removing clothes in the outdoors, the record buying public were still a conservative lot, especially for those over 30, who were teenagers in the 50s and now had young children. It was a record your 30 to 40 something parents bought in huge numbers, and they had more spare money than teenagers to do so. Also, I imagine if you were female (or gay), Engelbert was a top looking man especially if you wanted an alternative to Tom Jones. That must have helped with sales too.

However, the real claim to fame of this record is in its relation to the second place only chart standing of the Beatles' "Penny Lane/Strawberry Fields" single released at the same time in 1967. It could only get to No. 2 and is probably universally accepted as the greatest pair of songs to not hit the top spot. The double A sided songs were about Paul and John's childhood memories of geographical places in Liverpool, showing an evocative deeper thinking with the lyrics than just boy girl relationship issues. Yet in every chart going they only got to No. 2 because of the selling power of "Release Me". This is what gives Engelbert's single its unique selling point and why I wanted to include it in this book. It is likely that the clientele buying "Penny Lane/Strawberry Fields" were probably 10 years younger on average than those more elderly conservative types buying "Release Me". Yet there must have been a small crossover where some of the same fans bought both records and where the buyers actually liked all the songs. Whatever your or my views on "Release Me", or whether the song is "good, bad or ugly", it was able to keep two outstanding songs by common consent from being No. 1 and for that it deserves immense respect and a chapter all of its own here and now.

Engelbert on the back of "Release Me", carried on as a singing crooner, having hits and success across the world over the years. Perhaps the most bizarre event in his professional life was representing the UK at the Eurovision Song Contest in 2012 with the song "Love Will Set You Free". Unfortunately, it only achieved 25th place out of 26. Not that he would have worried, not being exactly strapped for cash as he has sold 140 million records in his career by 2024. At 87 he is still touring, still belting out the hits and was still officially bigger than the Beatles… for a few short weeks in 1967!

Chapter 5

The Good, the Bad and the Ugly: Hugo Montenegro

Released 11 September 1968
No. 1 for 4 weeks
13 November to 4 December '68
Sales UK: 200,000 approx.

There are three versions of "The Good, the Bad and the Ugly" (GBU): The first is a visual feast of epic proportions, then two are aural, one being a soundtrack and the other being a single that came out in 1968 and got to No. 1. The timeline goes something like this.

GBU: The Film came out in September 1966. This has already been mentioned in the Intro and only a quick précis is now in order. Three non-amigos go in search of gold and compete with each other to get it. The epic famous last scene shootout is iconic and memorable, suffice to say the (not quite so) good guy (Clint Eastwood) wins, defeating the bad guy (Lee Van Cleef) and the ugly guy (Eli Wallach). It was filmed in Spain in the summer of '66 and the bright, dry, dusty desertlike conditions just add to the atmosphere, literally and figuratively. The movie soundtrack was totally in sync with both the characters and the physical geography of the film. In my view it is one of the best cinematic efforts of visual and aural mixes ever. Even now, all these years later, you only need 10 seconds of music to be instantly transported back to remembering the film.

GBU: The Soundtrack was created for the film and unusually was part created before even the movie came out. The music first inspired the film rather than vice versa. Ennio Morricone, a regular collaborator with Sergio Leone the director, composed it. The main theme that would be covered for the 1968 single uses a "coyote sound" musical motif overall, but a different instrument to represent the three main protagonists, a flute for "good" Clint, an ocarina (a variation on a flute from South America) for "bad" Lee and human voices for "ugly" Eli, which made some "wah, wah" "go, go" and "who, who" noises as fabulous sound effects. This and the other music including the famous piece used over the final scene "The Ecstasy of Gold" are absolutely in my view just right for this film. If I hear the soundtrack music, I think of hot dusty desert only broken up by occasional tumbleweed plants. The music is geographically evocative as well as a lead in for the characters. You still hope the next time you watch the film "good" guy Clint still wins! The music was outstanding, could not be improved… or maybe the main theme could?

I had no idea in researching this chapter that the 1968 GBU: The Single was a cover. Does it improve on the original? It has the same musical motifs, violins, harmonica, whistling and an outstanding piccolo trumpet solo, so what was new by Hugo Montenegro compared to the original Ennio Morricone version? How about putting in some massed acoustic guitars to drive the rhythm, augmented by 4 beats to the bar, 4/4-time drums. Suddenly you could tap your feet to it and easily stay in time.

The record buying public loved GBU: The Single. It was preceded at No. 1 by Joe Cocker "With a Little Help from My Friends", a seriously intense Beatles cover from Sergeant Pepper and then afterward by "Lily the Pink" by the Scaffold, a well-written, entertainingly jokey song. In the middle was our instrumental, based on a theme from a 2-year-old film which sounded perhaps a little weird and unusual but still enchanted the teenagers and older types alike to get to No. 1 too.

No. 1 singles, of course, through our 45 trawls in this book can be eccentric and get away with it. For me, the blend of different instruments, non-lyrical voices and musical hooks was just so cool for my then 13-year-old self. And you could hum and "la, la" along even without any lyrics but just some vocal grunts. It also helped that there was a film tie in that had been a big success two years previously. GBU: The Single would perhaps have been a hit anyway because of its catchy melody.

Hugo Montenegro was an orchestral bandleader who reinterpreted others, doing film music covers and also wrote his own film scores. Apart from GBU: The Single, he is best known for composing the theme to the popular '60s spy thriller on TV "The Man from Uncle" He died in 1981 aged 55. He was a one hit wonder with "The Good, the Bad and the Ugly" but if you are to have only one hit, it is not a bad legacy.

Chapter 6

Je T'aime... Moi Non Plus: Jane Birkin and Serge Gainsbourg

Released 30 July 1969
No. 1 for 1 week
11 October '69
Sales UK: 250,000

Time for... a tongue in... cheek, (that's it) look at this most strange of No. 1s. The only single in our 45 45s with the immortal lyric line "entre mes reins", which translates literally to "between my kidneys". Just what were Jane and Serge up to? Well, it was not a medical procedure. Of all the songs in all the world, in all the time of the charts, this is one of the most eccentric, weird, wacky efforts of all time. It had sexualised lyrics, and heavy breathing in French but it got to No. 1 for one week only, but it still counts.

Serge Gainsbourg was a singer, songwriter, actor, composer and director known in France as a provocative purveyor of pop music. "Je T'aime... Moi Non Plus" (JT) was one of a mere 550 songs that he wrote in his lifetime. In 1967 he had a short relationship with Brigitte Bardot, who demanded he write the greatest love song ever for her, after a disappointing night out. So, Serge did, or at least made an attempt to do so. He recorded the first version of JT with Brigitte in attendance adding the female vocals. Rumour has it that this recording was peppered, (if that is the right word), with breathy vocalisations of a sexual nature not intended for children or adults of a nervous disposition. Gunter Sachs, Brigitte's husband at the time, kicked up such a fuss, along with Ms Bardot herself, that this version was not released then. It eventually came out in 1986.

Serge was very "frustrated" at this juncture (this is a difficult chapter to write without double entendres, so you may want to look away now) and was determined to get the record out. Luckily, he had a new girlfriend in 1968, English born Jane Birkin, who was more than happy to participate in a re-record that year. This new version of JT was to eventually come out in 1969.

The song title "Je T'Aime… Moi Non Plus" means literally "I Love You… Neither Do I". The best way to consider this title is something like this: "I love you, yes I do, I love you, yes I do, I love you, not any more (neither do I)" but… let's carry on anyway and it becomes sex without love… I think? An enigmatic, surreal title that has an air of mystery and a little confusion to it, which I am sure was deliberate on Serge's part. The lyrics with a little translation are perhaps easier to interpret and understand.

The record musically is organ led (oh dear!) with luscious strings, with a very hummable catchy melody. Lyrically well just where to begin? There is not much in the way of words, lots of "I love you", "neither do I" then some suggestive erotic lyrics such as "between my loins", all topped off climactically by the "between my kidneys" line. This could be inferred in a dramatic erotic fashion to mean something else entirely of a very sexualised nature, which I am not going to tell you about. I don't want this book only coming out after the watershed. Time to use your imagination or just go to the next chapter. The track is 4:22 minutes long, yet Jane's notorious heavy breathing does not arise (no) till 2:33 minutes. It subsides for a bit, then comes again (stop it!) right at the end. Although another famous myth about this song is that the end of version one of 1967 with Brigitte getting out of breath was spliced on to the Jane version of 1968.

And is it any wonder it got banned in virtually every country it was released in except France, where it could be played after 11pm.

I think of all the 45 songs in the list this is perhaps the most bizarre, though there are some other strong contenders to come in later years. Yet it became the first foreign language song to get to No. 1 and the first sex symbol, sorry sex single, to get to the top too.

The big question is why did it get to No. 1? Well, it had a nice catchy melody. It was a great song to have a close romantic sexy smooch to down at the disco. The English maybe did not understand all the racy lyrics and were therefore not offended too much. In the spirit of anything goes, late '60s rebellion then this was in its own way as freaky as Jimi Hendrix, so teenagers were buying it to be daring. And finally, there was a rumour, which I don't believe, that it was bought to make love to (especially by youngsters), who could possibly get by in 4:22 minutes! And good luck with that!

As a 14-year-old still obsessed by football, it rather passed me by. I was only aware of it in later years and having just listened to it again now for the book, I suppose for 1969, it was a little below the belt. For me, I still remain staggered that it got to No. 1.

Naturally there have been cover versions but luckily for all of us perhaps, they have been spoofs. From the hit comedy show "'Allo 'Allo!" actors Gordon Kaye and Vicki Michelle released a version in 1986. I remember watching it on TOTP, it was sort of embarrassing, the two "lovers" looked awkward. It got to No. 57 in the charts, not surprisingly 56 places lower than the original.

Serge Gainsbourg continued to release songs right up until his death in 1991 and has now achieved legendary status in French pop history. Jane Birkin divorced Serge in 1980 but stayed in France as an active actress and singer till her death in 2023. But of course, the pair are forever immortalised perhaps as one of the strangest No. 1s of all time and for that, their (lovemaking) legacy lives on.

Chapter 7

Back Home: England World Cup Squad

Released 18 April 1970
No. 1 for 3 weeks
16 May to 30 May '70
Sales UK: 250,00

If 1969 was the year of the sex song getting to No. 1, then 1970 was the year of the football song doing the same. Yet more evidence of just how fickle and dotty the charts were from year to year. Football is the No. 1 national sport in the UK, England and much of the world and along with sex and politics is also just about No. 1 casual talking point for many in the pub, street and household. I reckon football takes up about 20% of my conversation with my wife and friends, especially when I am getting really boring. It was just inevitable that eventually by 1970 an England football song would come out and probably get to No. 1.

If England had never won the World Cup in 1966, perhaps "Back Home" would never have come out. It was and still is the only time England had won it and was rightly celebrated at the time. I was 11 years old, about to become a spotty teenager, and I remember watching the game as if it was yesterday, on our smudgy black and white TV. All these years later I could still name the whole team, the most well-known three perhaps being Bobby Charlton, Bobby Moore and Geoff Hurst, the hat-trick goal scorer. These great players were still there in 1970 and the team were generally considered to be even better than that in '66. So how about a little musical encouragement for them and the fans, especially as it was going to be support at a distance, for the Cup was to be held in Mexico from 31st of May till 21st of June.

"Back Home" was ironically written by Phil Coulter, an Irishman, for the music and even more ironically by Bill Martin, a Scotsman, for the lyrics. It is unlikely they would have complained about the financial compensation in writing a football song for the "auld enemy". Between 1967 and 1976 they were the "go to" writers of the day if you wanted chart success with a light pop song. Other biggies at No. 1 from them included "Puppet on a String" by Sandie Shaw, which won Eurovision in 1967 and "Congratulations" by Cliff Richard, which could only muster 2nd place at Eurovision in '68. By the time "Back Home" came out in 1970, the football team could only finish joint 5th (beaten quarter finalists) in the World Cup. It was a downward spiral for Coulter and Martin, and they must take the blame for England's earlier than expected demise. I jest, as on the UK singles charts, they all got to No. 1.

The song got to No. 1 for three weeks in May 1970, which was in the build-up period to the World Cup, which started at the end of May. It was a chart topper in anticipation of a victory. However, when this song was No. 1 back home in England, captain Bobby Moore had been arrested in Columbia on the warmup tour, accused of stealing a bracelet. He was eventually released after four days without charge and went back to Mexico to join the rest of the squad in time for the first game. I wonder if this incident helped with later sales, as fans bought the record in solidarity and sympathy.

"Back Home" as a song was only 2:07 minutes long, one of the shortest in our list of 45 45s. I remember the players in bow ties and suits, singing along in the Top of the Pops studio, all looking vaguely embarrassed. Their vocals were all recorded to sound deep and manly in a pub singer sort of way, all in tune but with not a hint of harmony. They certainly were not the Beach Boys. Lyrically the words are an ode to the fans back home, where the team realise they are being watched on TV, will do their best and not let the nation down. In reality, England played well, but in the quarterfinals, they were ahead 2-0 when

Alf Ramsey pulled off Bobby Charlton to rest their star player for the semi-final. West Germany then pulled three goals back, won the game and got their revenge for 1966. The thought is, of course, if England had won the World Cup in 1970 "Back Home" would no doubt have resurged itself back up to the top of the charts and stayed at No. 1 for ever, well, probably to September. As that did not happen, we should be grateful perhaps, as we got Mungo Jerry's "In the Summertime" for six weeks, then Elvis Presley with "The Wonder of You" for seven weeks instead, up to September.

For my 14-year-old self, "Back Home" was ok but not a patch on two further No. 1 singles by or about the England football team to come. "Three Lions" by the Lightning Seeds and Skinner and Baddiel, out originally in 1996 for the England based Euros. It was a great effort with the iconic "It's coming home" chorus. However, my personal favourite was from 1990 with New Order and The England World Cup Squad "World in Motion", this being the one with the John Barnes rap. Both these songs though did get England to the semi-finals, which make them a definite improvement on "Back Home", which only got the team to the quarters. However, the 1970 effort was an obvious No. I. It's foot-tappable, sing-alongable, and helped to build up the excitement for the World Cup for a football mad country. It does sound rather dated now in a way that the other two songs do not.

Most of the singers on Back Home have sadly passed away including the two Bobbys, Moore and Charlton. Geoff Hurst is still going strong well into his '80s, still happy to talk about 1966 and 1970. Just don't ask him to sing "Back Home".

Chapter 8

Grandad: Clive Dunn

Released 10th November 1970
No. 1 for 3 weeks
9 January to 23 January '71
Sales UK: 772,000

And now for something completely different... again! Take a middle-aged man pretending to be old and decrepit, and the bass player who played the amazing strutting walking bass line on Lou Reed's "Walk on the Wild Side". Add in the lead singer from a late 1960s psychedelic rock band and then put them together and hey presto, you have a novelty children's song. How did they do it? It never ceases to amaze me how some of the songs in the book come together and yet somehow end up at No. 1.

In January '71 Clive Dunn had his 51st birthday. In reality, he was fit, healthy and fully able to do the physical stunts undertaken in Dad's Army, which the other elderly actors in it could not do. He had been playing the very much past it, doddery, confused Corporal Jones in the famous Home Guard BBC sitcom for three years from 1968, to great acclaim. He could easily become an obviously aged figure to play a stereotypical Grandad for a new musical venture. In the film of TOTP, he sits there in his rocking chair in flat cap and old mac, remembering the golden old days in song. His grandchildren look up to him admiringly and sing, "Grandad you're lovely". The problem was that for millions of people watching they were really singing, "Grandad you're ugly" (Well that's what it sounded like to me!). At the end Grandad nods off, overwhelmed with the effort of singing the song. After that no doubt Clive woke up and was still young enough in real life to run all the way to the bank. In 2024 the video has a definite creepy air about it – it could not be made now.

Meanwhile writer Herbie Flowers was the bass player in Blue Mink. Later in the classical/rock crossover band Sky, he was virtuoso enough to play bass for them too. As a session player of some renown, he also played tuba. He appeared mainly as a bass player on records by Elton John and David Bowie, amongst others, but in particular on "Transformer" by Lou Reed, which included "Walk on the Wild Side" in 1972.

Kenny Pickett, the cowriter had been the vocalist in '60s prototype, progressive, psychedelic rock group The Creation. One day he came round to visit Herbie, rang the doorbell and created a No. 1 record.

Herbie had been given a book on simple composition and then had written a rather sad melancholy tune. Legend has it Kenny visited and rang the doorbell, which gave Herbie the musical motif or hook to complete the musical track for "Grandad". Kenny wrote the lyrics, and the rest is (sort of) history.

The song is in a shuffling waltz time, being piano led, accompanied by strings, with a hint of Herbie's tuba every now and then. "Good old days" words and the "you're lovely/(ugly)" refrain make up the lyrics. Clive sings really well, very clearly enunciating the words, giving the lyrics a pathos melancholic feel.

So, who was buying this? Mums and dads for young children, and perhaps mums and dads for their own parents, must have been doing so. Also, everyone in between was also buying it as well, but just not admitting it. I was now just about a teenager in 1971 and I hated it with a passion. It was just not cool. My own male grandparents were not remotely like that. I found them scary and remote, but they were of their stiff upper lip time, and they meant well. Now I appreciate it as a nice little tune but the old man with little girls video TOTP film is a definite non-starter for 2024. The song has, I suppose, a certain period charm and is by no means the worst in our 45 45s.

Clive Dunn eventually had a children's TV show called Grandad which ran on ITV from 1979 to '84 from whence he retired to go and live in Portugal. He died in 2006 aged 85. Herbie Flowers is alive, well and retired, last making a jazz album in 2012. Kenny Pickett continued making music until his death in 1997, aged 55.

Chapter 9

Telegram Sam: T. Rex

Released 21 January 1972
No. 1 for 2 weeks
5 February to 12 February '72
Sales UK: 200,000 approx.

In 1971, at the end of T. Rex's monster hit "Get It On", Marc Bolan says, "meanwhile I'm still thinking" and that much was very true with what was to come, as they were halfway through their sequence of four No. 1s. It started off with "Hot Love" and then "Get It On" in 1971, then was carried on into 1972 by "Telegram Sam" and "Metal Guru". There were also, amazingly, four No. 2 hits as well: "Ride a White Swan" in 1970, "Jeepster" in 1971, with "Children of the Revolution" and "Solid Gold Easy Action" in 1972. "20th Century Boy" got to No. 3 in 1973. In total, they had eleven top 10 hits over three years. You could say T. Rex were showing a bit of promise and doing quite well and having the "biggest pop group in the UK" status during this time.

Marc Bolan was born in 1947 and had been around the musical block a few times prior to this 1970s excitement. He was briefly part of a shock rock band in the mid '60s called John's Children, who at one time had put out an album called Orgasm! Naturally it got banned and did not sell. By 1967 he decided to downsize the wild image and be a hippy dippy pixie in an acoustic duo called Tyrannosaurus Rex with percussion and bongo player Steve Took. They were championed by alternative Radio 1 DJ John Peel and had some limited commercial success. Some of this music is light, whimsical, full of Eastern and British folk influences and is not half bad. It gives little indication of what is to come.

By 1969, as Tyrannosaurus Rex was such a mouthful and difficult to spell, Marc decided to shorten the name to T. Rex and be less hippy dippy and more rock'n'roll. New percussion and bongo player Mickey Finn came in, augmented by bassist Steve Currie and drummer Bill Legend. "Ride a White Swan" was the breakthrough hit in 1970, followed by the two massive ones in '71 ("Hot Love", "Get It On") with a popular No. 2 in "Jeepster" and then in early '72 to our song "Telegram Sam".

By this date Marc and T. Rex were hot property and could do no wrong. A combination of sing-along songs, hummable choruses, with great bluesy foot-tapping rock arrangements were the key. There was also Marc as a fashion coat hanger in wearing outrageous feminine clothing, velvet and satin suits that proved to be the birth of glam rock, which added to their appeal. Marc especially and the band also became incredibly popular with girls. It was Beatlemania all over again! Marc, in particular, was not complaining. He had always wanted to be a star and got there first, before his good friend David Bowie. By the mid-70s though, David had most definitely caught up.

"Telegram Sam" is a fascinating single. It is very nearly a copy of "Get It On" and has some wonderfully entertaining and humorous lyrics. Musically it was the same chord sequence as "Get It On" but in a different key of A, rather than E. The song was about Marc's manager Tony Secunda who was the "main man" in the song. Other interpretations are that the song is about a messenger who brought Marc a telegram (pre-email/texts) that said "Get It On" had got to No. 1. Yet the song is populated by some great other characters, such as Golden Nose Slim, Jungle Faced Jake and Purple Pie Pete. The Bobby character could be a reference to Bob Dylan. All mysterious and enigmatic lyrics. However, one line that is easily comprehensible is "I ain't no square with my corkscrew hair", which is my favourite lyric of the song.

I was 15 when this came out. I was a TOTP addict and very aware of T. Rex and sort of a fan. I adored "Get It On" and

"Jeepster" and constantly looked in the mirror to see if my longer wavy hair would have a go at going corkscrew. Sadly, it didn't. "Telegram Sam" for me was ok but it was a bit samey and even with my limited musical intelligence I saw it as a copy of "Get It On". Still, if you are going to copy and rip anybody off you may as well do it to yourself.

Why was Telegram Sam a success? All the previously mentioned T. Rex attributes are still in play here, but I think the main reason was the momentum built up during the run of hits in 1971, which meant there was an oven ready record buying public for any new T. Rex release in '72. Also, there were the great entertaining lyrics, which Marc sang quite clearly and was backed up vocally by Howard Kaylan, Mark Volman and producer Tony Visconti.

There was a great cover (in my view) of Telegram Sam by the gothic punk group Bauhaus in 1979. It has a very funny mock horror video, which I think is brilliantly ridiculous. But it is not everybody's cup of tea. It did not chart here but did get to No. 12 in the charts in New Zealand for good measure.

After this, Marc Bolan and T. Rex slowed right down commercially, so by 1977 they could hardly sell any records. Like many before and after, they had had their day and gone out of fashion. Friend and rival David Bowie was so good this never really happened to him, becoming an all-time great. However, in 1977 Marc was hosting a six-part TV series called "Marc" which had created a revival of interest in him from the public. One of the last artists to sing with him on the show was David Bowie. Sadly, on the 16th of September 1977 Marc Bolan was a passenger in a car driven by his girlfriend Gloria Jones, which hit a tree in Barnes, South London. He was killed instantly. He was only 29.

Of the other players, Mickey Finn died in 2003 of liver failure and Steve Currie died in 1979 in a car accident in Portugal. Bill Legend is still going strong and is the only person who got to No. 1 in this book who I have actually met. I knew him for a while in the 1990s. He was a great drummer, very professional, very understated as a personality and a very nice chap.

It was a great loss when Marc died, he appeared to be back on the way up and we will never know what might have been. There is a (sort of) happy ending. The T. Rex band of 1971-72: Marc, Mickey, Steve, and Bill were inducted into the Rock & Roll Hall of Fame in 2020.

Chapter 10

Cum On Feel the Noize: Slade

Released 23 February 1973
No. 1 for 4 weeks
3 March to 24 March '73
Sales UK: 500,000

In early 1972 as a 16-year-old, I attended my first ever live concert at the Trent Polytechnic in Nottingham. The band struggled to get the cool, possibly stoned, university students to get up and dance but they very much succeeded with me and my peer group of friends, as we jumped up and down and headbanged our way through their set. We then had to run across Nottingham to the bus station to get the last bus home. The problem was, the band were so loud that I could not hear properly for about an hour afterwards. The last bus was very quiet, I could see people talking but I just couldn't hear them. What a great first concert! The band was of course Slade. You may just have heard of them!

By this time Slade had had their first No. 1 "Coz I Luv You". They went on to have five other No. 1s including our featured song and the perennial Christmas favourite "Merry Xmas Everybody" that sold over a million copies. Between '71 and '74 they had twelve top 5 singles, far outselling T. Rex. Through the '70s they managed to sell more singles than anyone else even including ABBA.

The band formed in 1966 and eventually morphed from Ambrose Slade to just Slade by 1969. In that year they went with a skinhead image but new manager Chas Chandler, ex bass player in the Animals and also Jimi Hendrix's manager, asked them to grow it out, as the look was associated with football hooligans. The four members were Noddy Holder on lead vocals and guitar, Dave Hill on lead guitar and soon to be glamorously silly outfits, Jim Lea on bass and violin and Don Powell on drums. Noddy and Jim wrote the songs. As skinheads, they looked the business. Noddy in particular was not someone you would want to upset. Even with long hair they never looked cuddly (well maybe apart from Dave who quite often looked like a teddy bear in satin). The image was mainly tough, working class, of the people with the common touch. This was exaggerated more when; to the bane of teachers everywhere they started to misspell their song titles. They had a had a top 20 hit with "Get Down and Get with It" in June 1971 but the breakthrough hit, and first misspelling was "Coz I Luv You" at the end of '71.

Throughout '72, as well as giving me partial deafness, they consolidated their position as the best pop/rock band around, usurping T. Rex, whose peak was about a year earlier, with some great songs and numerous TOTP appearances. By early 1973 a campaign to allow "Cum On Feel the Noize" to be played on the radio before release meant it was already familiar to the punters and it went straight into the charts at No. 1, an achievement not replicated since the Beatles got straight to the top spot with "Get Back" in 1969.

The track, instrumentally, is very well produced, with pounding drums, handclaps and neat little guitar interludes. In other words, it was heavy rock/pop suitable for air guitarists and headbangers everywhere. But it is the vocals that really do it. Noddy's voice was terrifyingly good, one of the best rock vocalists ever. After the sad demise of singer Bon Scott from AC/DC in 1980, The Nodd nearly joined that band. Imagine that, with Noddy singing "Back in Black" (however, Brian Johnson came in as a brilliant replacement for Bon anyway).

Lyrically the words were there to capture the excitement of a live performance by Slade, where you just go wild and have a great time. While all in the UK loved the song, it did nothing in the USA until Quiet Riot did a definite metallish rock cover in 1983 that got to No. 5 in the Billboard charts. Listening to it as I write, it is not a patch on Noddy and the lads. The song was also revived by Oasis as a live cover in their concerts in the '90s. Put the wall of "noize" guitars to one side and Liam's and Noel's vocals are "shouty" and commendable.

Slade were only to have two more No. 1s, with "Skweeze Me, Pleeze Me" (top misspelling) and the Christmas one over the 1973 festivities and then rather like T. Rex before them they faded away as fashions changed. In the early '80s they had a mini revival as a heavy metal band but finally retired gracefully into middle age in 1992.

"Cum On Feel the Noize" is a great, great song! I loved it at the time and still do now. It was bouncy, fun, uplifting with amazing playing and singing only Noddy can do. No wonder it was a deserving No. 1. If only they could spell…

Noddy Holder post-1992 moved on to TV work with roles and cameos here, there and everywhere. He remains universally popular. Jim Lea retrained as a psychotherapist but mainly lives a quiet life. Dave Hill carried on in Slade 11, still playing the hits, which now continues as just Slade to this day. Finally, a real thought for Don Powell who on the 4th of July 1973 had a road accident that severely injured him and killed his girlfriend, Angela Morris. Don has suffered short-term memory loss and some sensing issues but through his drive and determination was able to come back and play the drums. Post-1992 he played in Slade 11 with Dave, but sadly this stopped in 2020 when Dave asked him to leave… by email!

Slade leave a great pop rock legacy. For three years they were unstoppable at the very top and somewhere at some time in the world, Noddy Holder is forever throwing away his dictionary and belting out "Cum On Feel the Noize".

Chapter 11

Billy Don't Be a Hero: Paper Lace

Released 23 February 1974
No. 1 for 3 weeks
16 March to 30March '74
Sales UK: 200,000 approx.

I picked this song, as the band came from Nottingham, my hometown, and in 1974 I knew someone, who knew someone, who knew the band, as you do. Nottingham has hardly been a hotbed of new fantastic pop music over the years, unlike Manchester, Liverpool or Birmingham. London tends to lead with artists because of its very much larger population. From there would come the Rolling Stones, T. Rex, Queen and Elton John from performers on our 45 list, while Liverpool had a cute little pop combo called the Beatles, who showed some promise. Slade were Birmingham, Wet Wet Wet were from Scotland, The Wurzels were from Somerset, Robbie Williams was from Stoke on Trent/Manchester, while Mr Blobby probably just fell out the sky.

In terms of acts mainly not on the 45 list of No. 1s or who scored high-ranking chart success, consider Manchester. Try the Hollies in the '60s, 10cc in the '70s and in the '80s and '90s take your pick from the Smiths, New Order, Simply Red, most of Take That, the Stone Roses and Oasis on our list for the 1995 No. 1 "Some Might Say". This puts Nottingham and most other cities well in the shade.

The only other significant band from Nottingham was Ten Years After, a bluesy rock outfit with whiz kid guitar player Alvin Lee (sadly passed away 2013). They never released any singles but had some album success. Which gets us up to date in 2024 with modern pop star Jake Bugg from Nottingham and that's about it. Apart from Paper Lace, nearly but not quite one hit wonders.

The band were formed in 1967 as Music Box, soon changing to Paper Lace (lace being a major product made in Nottingham). They played semi-professionally for a few years and by 1973 had gravitated to Opportunity Knocks on ITV, which they won five weeks in a row. Professional songwriters Mitch Murray and Peter Callander, looking for a new band to foster and promote, gave "Billy Don't Be a Hero" to Paper Lace, which promptly made No. 1 in March 1973. Mitch wrote the music and Peter did the lyrics and they had already penned several hits such as "Even the Bad Times Are Good" for the Tremeloes and "Goodbye Sam, Hello Samantha" for Cliff Richard. Peter sadly passed away some years ago, but Mitch is still going strong as a comedy after dinner speaker, a quite unexpected career change. Slightly after this in May '74, they also gave "Billy" to an American band Bo Donaldson and the Heywoods, who also got their virtually identical version to No. 1 in the Billboard American charts on the 15th of June 1974. Paper Lace did release their "Billy" version, which needless to say was only a very minor hit, getting to No. 96 in the Billboard chart. That would, however, change dramatically with Paper Lace's next USA single!

Lyrically it's a song asking Billy, a soldier who is going to war, to not be a hero and come back alive. At the end of the song Billy's fiancée reads a letter saying he died a hero, but she then throws the letter away in disgust. An anti-war song! The lyrics actually become quite powerful with the last "punch line", surpassing perhaps the quality of the musical track. Paper Lace wore American Civil War Union uniforms on TOTP, but it could also be interpreted as being about Vietnam, therefore creating rather a strange link with our 1985 song "19", which was the average age of American soldiers in the Vietnam War. Another anti-war song!

Musically it is a bit nondescript, some marching drums, some nice whistling and ok singing from drummer vocalist Phil Wright. Much as I tried to like this song in solidarity with my fellow Nottingham brothers, I just couldn't, but then the next single was a distinct improvement with a lot more bite musically.

It cannot feature in this book; it only got to No. 3 in the UK in May '74 but did top the charts in the USA. "The Night Chicago Died" was about a very fictional shootout between Al Capone and the Police. It was a dubious story inaccurate in reality but had a great catchy tune. Later in 74 "The Black-Eyed Boys" got to No. 11 and then in 1978 "We've Got the Whole World in Our Hands" was a combined effort with Nottingham Forest FC, stalling at No. 28 and that was it for Paper Lace.

The band members in 1974 were Phil Wight: lead vocals/drums, Mick Vaughn: lead guitar, Cliff Fish: bass, Chris Morris: guitar/vocals and Carlo Santanna: guitar/vocals (his real name; not to be confused with Carlos Santana the Latin American classic rock guitar hero). They kept going until 1984, split up, reformed, etc like many of the bands, post-fame, featured in this book. Cliff Fish, the bass player unfortunately died in 2023; the rest are still alive and kicking.

So why was it such a big hit? A nice light tune to hum to, lyrics that tell a story with an anti-war message and for me it almost has a children's song appeal and maybe it was bought for teenagers, especially girls, who would have been enchanted with the (slightly soppy) romanticism of the lyrics. It just goes to show the record buying public were still very diverse in their tastes in the '70s. You still never quite knew what could get to No. 1. An opera (sort of) was going to be our chosen No. 1 next year in 1975. Who would have thought?

Paper Lace had their year in the sun and like or loath "Billy", as soon as you hear the marching drums and whistling, you know what is coming.

Chapter 12

Bohemian Rhapsody: Queen

Released 8 November 1975
No. 1 for 9 weeks
6 December '75 to 24 January '76
Sales UK: 2.6m

In 2013 I went with my now wife to pick up her 16-year-old daughter and her friend from a night out. Both girls were a little tipsy but that did not stop them singing "Bohemian Rhapsody" all the way home. They knew every single word, especially the opera section, and then air guitared the guitar solo in fits of giggles. There was no music on the CD player; they just knew the song backwards oh so well. Both girls were born in 1998, 23 years after "Bo Rhap" first got to No. 1. After the death of Freddie Mercury, it had got to No. 1 again in late 1991 but this is still seven years before their births. Yet everyone just seems to know "Bo Rhap". It seems to be part of our collective consciousness. It is the best-known song, the most talked and written about song, and possibly the best song of all in our 45 45s. Some would argue the best ever song, perhaps? All done and dusted in just under six minutes.

Let's start with the birth of Queen. Brian May: guitar/vocals, Roger Taylor: drums/vocals and Freddie Mercury: lead vocals/piano got together as Queen in 1970, being joined by John Deacon: bass in 1971. They could be described in the early days as a heavy rock group in the vein of perhaps Led Zeppelin and Deep Purple, but what made them different, even then, were the vocals and the fantastic harmonies. Their second hit in October 1974, "Killer Queen" (No. 2) was a real breakthrough having all the typical ingredients of Classic Queen: a catchy melody, entertaining lyrics, clear and distinct vocals from Freddie with additional harmonies, while retaining the heavy rock element with pounding drums from Roger and a cute little guitar solo from Brian. It was all set up for the biggie the following year.

Freddie wrote "Bo Rhap" but the whole band plus producer Roy Thomas Baker were involved in developing and arranging the track. It was cobbled together from three song fragments Freddie had and would eventually be segregated into six distinct sections over just under six minutes. This made it rather symphonic in classical terms. It had no "verse chorus" format. Of the other No. 1s in this book, it is perhaps a similar musical multistage concept to "Good Vibrations" from the Beach Boys in 1966, but very definitely not similar for the lyrics. It could also be considered as a piece of prog rock having a segmented approach with twists and turns similar to "suite pieces" by bands such as Yes or Jethro Tull. Yet it ended up as No. 1 single for nine weeks.

Let's start with the musical track. Then I will be taking a week off to rest before tackling the lyrics. A very nice Intro (the six sections are started with capital letters) with great harmonies and piano playing takes us up to 49 seconds, where the Ballad section goes on to 2:37 minutes. So far, a nice song, probably not going to be remembered forever at this point to 2:37 minutes then augmented by a wonderfully fluid Brian Guitar Solo to 3:05 minutes when the Opera starts.

All I can say is "Wow" about the Operatic segment! As no doubt others did, when first hearing it, with just three singers involved (John Deacon did not sing and was away having his lunch, but he may as well have gone on holiday). It took the best part of three weeks in mid-1975 to record the vocal harmony track by Freddie (middle bits), Roger (high bits) and Brian (lower bits) consisting in the end of 180 overdubs. The feeling is that this section goes on forever, but it only lasts for 1:02 minutes to 4:07 minutes. The last few seconds as the harmony vocals rise up and build the tension to the Hard Rock riff that follows is brilliant, then it's headbanging time all round. This bit always reminds me of the great "Bo Rhap" scene in the 1992 film Wayne's World, where the singing in the car turns into headbanging at that moment. At 4:55 minutes it quietens down for the Outro, similar to the Intro. And only a song like this could finish with a massive gong!

OK, lyrics time, here goes. The protagonist in the story kills a man and has to face up to his demons. In the Opera the subject is in despair "nobody loves me" and he is very much portrayed as a victim. By the end of the Outro "nothing really matters" and do I care because "anyway the wind blows" and the protagonist gets over it. That is the short version analysis of the lyrics. You can find seriously in-depth meanderings and musings on the words in books and the internet, if you so desire. Freddie never said what they meant anyway, and it might have been all nonsense. Certainly, in prog rock circles being enigmatic and weird with lyrics that no one really understood was a full-time hobby, just ask Jon Anderson, then of Yes. Yet "Bo Rhap" still ended up at nine weeks at No. 1. Just why?

It was something different from the usual simplistic No. 1 songs and people would have found it far more challenging as a listen, but ultimately more rewarding. Classical music types who had never bought a single before might have just bought it for the Opera section. The melodies are catchy, the rock bits are there for the rockers, and the lyrics may or may not be nonsense, but they are wonderfully entertaining. It is great to sing along to with friends at karaoke or even on your own. When the Opera finishes and the Hard Rock guitar riff starts is one of the best tension diffusing, release moments of all time in any record ever. There is something there for everyone! It was wonderfully well produced and played with virtuoso instrumental intensity, but for me the singing with harmonies, especially in the Opera, give "Bo Rhap" its unique selling point. I admit, even as a middle-aged man, playing air guitar to the Hard Rock section.

Freddie's friend Kenny Everett, '70s DJ, was given a prerelease single and at Capital Radio played the song in segments and then in total 14 times in two days to build up demand just before release. Critics were not impressed, saying it was too long, too prog rock, no chorus, etc, but they were wrong. It was also promoted by the well-known "four singing heads" music video which cost £4,500 and took four hours to make, which pioneered the use of short films for promotion. When it was released in late 1991 following Freddie's death, it still returned to No. 1 for five weeks. It was played live by Queen over the years in segments, with the Opera played from the record while the band nipped off stage to count the royalties. The feature film about Freddie from 2018, Bohemian Rhapsody, only enhanced its reputation.

Queen carried on being one of the best rock pop bands of all time till Freddie's sad death aged 45 from Aids in 1991. Brian and Roger have carried on with Queen in the 21st century with vocalists Paul Rodgers and Adam Lambert. John Deacon has retired and is something of a recluse.

It is certainly Freddie's and Queen's greatest song, if not one of the greatest songs of all time. It is absolutely staggering to compare this epic with some of the other mixed-up No. 1s in this book, which I have deliberately picked to provide a contrast to songs like this. Not to mention any names… but maybe we only have to look one year ahead.

Chapter 13

The Combine Harvester (Brand New Key): The Wurzels

Released 15 May 1976
No. 1 for 2 weeks
12 June to 19 June '76
Sales UK: 250,000

From the sublime to the sublimely ridiculous, perhaps? It is always time for another comedy song to put a smile on our faces, confound the critics and prove anything can sell. If a No. 1 can "do the fandango" in 1975, then an everyday tale of a farmer exchanging a combine harvester for the lady's hand in marriage, while collecting an extra 43 acres of good arable land in the process, can do so well in 1976. That is what it was like in our crazy mixed up pop charts.

It all started in 1972 when American folky, hippy singer-songwriter Melanie (Melanie Anne Safka Schekeryk, to give her full name) put out a song called "Brand New Key", where a girl on roller skates tries to get the attention of a boy she rather fancies. Musically it has a country feel with piano and banjo to the fore, was a No. 1 in the Billboard charts and sold 3m copies across the world, over the end of '71 going into '72. It got to No. 4 in the UK charts.

Meanwhile on another (part of the) planet there arose in 1967 an entertainingly strange band of West Country Somerset locals or yokels called the Wurzels. They soon had songs about drinking cider, and spreading cow dung, probably at the same time, all worthy countryside pursuits. The main man and songwriter was Adge Cutler, who wrote original songs on these themes, but he was sadly to die in 1974 in a road accident. By 1976 the three main remaining band members, Tommy Banner,

Peter Budd and Tony Baylis had decided the way forward was to take popular songs with rewritten lyrics to take account of the West Country, farming machinery, drinking and romantic traditions all appreciated by Wurzelites everywhere.

Simultaneously, over in Ireland a chap called Brendan O'Shaughnessy had taken Melanie's "Brand New Key" and rewritten the words to be put out as a single. This was "Combine Harvester (Brand New Key)" by Brendan Grace, which topped the Irish charts. So, it was this cover by the Wurzels, of a cover by Brendan Grace of Melanie's original, that became the No. 1 record in the UK. So, our "Combine" was a cover of a cover, which must make it a double cover, "twice removed". It spent two weeks at No. 1 and made a lot of people very happy.

Musically it was similar to Melanie's version with banjo and piano augmented by an entertaining addition of a growling tuba. Lyrically the lyrics are... well funnyish, going along something like this: "I have only got 20 acres you have 43, marry me, give me your acreage and you can have the combine". A cunning plan as if they got married, he would presumably have access to the combine anyway. It was also a sensible plan to increase productivity. Bigger arable farms, more crops and more mechanisation with subsidies from the European Economic Community were definitely the way forward in the '70s for a lot of farmers. Was it pro-EEC political song then? I think not! Anyway, 54 lines of lyrics were probably quite enough to explain that the farmer wanted it all, more land and the girl, while cleverly keeping the combine.

The Wurzels got to No. 3 in September '76 with "I Am a Cider Drinker" based on "Paloma Blanca", originally done by the George Baker Selection and that was it more or less for hits. "Combine" was rereleased in 2001, only getting to No. 39. The Wurzels carried on releasing albums, changing personnel and entertaining with live gigs in the 21st century. My favourite moment of their post "Combine" career is when they put out an album out in 2002 called "Never Mind The Bullocks, Ere's The

Wurzels" a spoof on the infamous Sex Pistols album of a similar name, of which I am sure you can guess. Of the three members who played and sang on "Combine" Tommy and Peter are still going strong. Tony Baylis sadly passed away in 2020.

    Did I like the song? Absolutely not, but I can hazard a guess or three why it became a No. 1 hit. The music is twee, light and simple but the lyrics are funnily ridiculous. However, there were words that people could sort of relate to involving love, sex, acquisition of property including vehicles and land. Also being set in a West Country farm setting and sung all in a silly accent would have helped. At the end of the day, it is for a lot of people a very entertaining song. I have tried my best when playing it for this book to suppress a grin, but it has not worked. The Opera section of "Bo Rhap" makes me grin too, it just has better harmonies. Am I saying the two songs have equal status? No, I am not, but the great British public made both songs No. 1 in 1975 and '76 respectively and that is the bottom line! What a funny thing the charts were… and not much was going to change for another 30 years.

Chapter 14

Knowing Me, Knowing You: ABBA

Released 26 February 1977
No. 1 for 5 weeks
2 April to 30 April '77
Sales UK: 976,000

It would be difficult to do a book of this sort and leave ABBA out. Are they the greatest pop group of all time? Many would think so. While the Beatles by 1967 moved into rock, having conceptualised albums like Sergeant Pepper and complex lyrics about metaphorical walruses, ABBA stuck to their winning formula throughout. They had lyrics about relationships, wonderful melodies with classical flourishes, great singing with luscious harmonies and tap along disco rhythms. There was no go to concept album and no prog rock flourishes. It was a simple idea and it worked …. big time for eight years!

Between early 1974 and late 1981 they had 19 top ten hits, of which nine were No. 1s. This amounted to 11.3m single sales in the UK. Over a lifetime they have shifted up to 385m records worldwide. Their music is ubiquitously everywhere, part of the ether. Yet they started off as a twee little Swedish folk group no one outside of that country was ever going to hear of. But thanks to the magic of Eurovision…

ABBA were Agnetha Fältskog, Björn Ulvaeus, Benny Andersson and Anni-Frid Lyngstad. In order, this was the super sexy blonde bombshell who everybody fancied (not me, I am saving my affection for Kate Bush in the next chapter), the clean-shaven guitar player, the bearded piano player and the auburn-haired female singer. Eurovision in 1974 was their breakthrough with "Waterloo", more pop than folk and sung in English, which became their first No. 1 in the UK. Then there was a slight fade to July 1975, when "SOS" came out and only got to No 6. I was

20 at the time, about to go to university and far too cool, man, to like ABBA. An admission of liking such groups would destroy one's "street cred" in my peer group. However, my younger early teenage brother did buy the record, which I can now admit all these years later, that I actually used to play when he was not looking because I really thought "SOS" was great! It even sounded heavy, not quite Deep Purple but showing a guitar riff promise. After this "Mamma Mia", and "Fernando" quickly followed at No. 1 despite my refusal to personally buy their singles, followed by the biggest of the big. "Dancing Queen" in 1976 was huge everywhere and was their only single to get to the top of the Billboard charts in America. Is DQ the greatest pop song of all time? Everything that made ABBA special is there, great lyrical hooks, wonderful melody, a sing-along danceable groove and it makes you feel good inside. It had no pretensions to be a mini symphony in 6 parts. And to think I picked a song ahead of it for 1976 about arable farming, well I never!

But forward to 1977 and just maybe to ABBA's 2nd or 3rd best song "Knowing Me, Knowing You". After a slight blip with a No. 3 for "Money, Money, Money" in November 1976, "Knowing" came out in February '77 and got to No. 1 by April of that year for five weeks. It was a classic relationship break up song as the paired couples in the band, Agnetha and Björn followed by Benny and Anni-Frid, were both having relationship difficulties. I cannot help thinking of the similar break up issues affecting Fleetwood Mac at the same time. They also produced a fantastic set of separating songs such as "Go Your Own Way" put out on the album Rumours and broke up all the way to the bank. There is no doubt that these sad circumstances can produce great music of artistic merit and "Knowing" has a sad pathos and melancholic feel which very much enhances it.

Having just listened to the song, while watching the video after a long time, has nearly moved me to tears but not quite. The music is exquisite, wonderfully produced, but the vocals with harmonies and the counterpoint singing melody by the two men is a real highlight. The lyrics with all the issues about break ups are very straightforward and very sad. I am not sure about the repeated "ah ha's" during the song though, they sound a bit comedic, and lend themselves to Jim's famous scene in The Vicar of Dibley.

By 1977 a successful video could very much enhance the reputation of a song and increase sales and that is true here. There were lots of meaningful looks, broken hugs and the girls walking away at the end into the snow in the video. Very brave really as the four principals were not acting at the time.

So finally, after all these years I can now own up, as many others have, to liking ABBA. I get their musical and lyrical genius, and this is a great song. Perhaps the greatest break up song of all time? I just may have to listen to the song again for its emotional hit even after I finish this chapter. It is very obvious why this song resonated so much with so many people as everybody (nearly) breaks up sometime.

ABBA carried on at the height of success for a few more years post "Knowing". My favourite single was "Gimme! Gimme! Gimme! (A Man After Midnight)". They sort of petered out by 1982 and while Björn and Benny then worked with Tim Rice on the musical Chess, the girls did bits here and there musically but kept a lower profile. In the early '90s the ABBA-esque single by Erasure renewed interest, so that by '99 the Mama Mia musical came along followed by the film of the same name in 2008. ABBA Voyage, the 9th album of new songs, was eventually released in 2021 but come May 2022 there was the most startling development of all. You could see ABBA nearly live. The technical phrase is a virtual concert experience performed by motion captured digital avatars (or Abbatars) as the foursome were in 1979. This is performed at the ABBA Arena at the Queen Elizabeth Olympic Park in East London and is of course absolutely abbamazing (oh dear)!

So, what is ABBA's greatest song? Smooth radio in 2023 put "Knowing" in 3rd place behind "The Winner Takes It All" and DQ. It is the 3rd biggest seller behind DQ (1m+) and Super Trouper (982,000) with (976,000). In my own list Gimme! Gimme! Gimme! would be first, then DQ then "Knowing". However, in the context of this mixed up book the song must be right up there as one of the best of the 45 45s featured.

Chapter 15

Wuthering Heights: Kate Bush

Released 20ʰ January 1978
No. 1 for 4 weeks
11 March to 1 April '78
Sales UK: 600,000

Kate Bush is unique, an absolute one-off, there being no one quite like her, before or since. National treasure springs to mind very much in the vein of people like Stephen Fry and Billy Connolly but perhaps not Mr Blobby, who like everybody else has told me in our correspondence, that he is a fan of Kate. In a 46-year career she only had nine UK top 10 albums and only played live in one tour in 1979 and then during a residency of 22 shows at the Hammersmith Apollo in 2014. Yet mention Kate Bush to anybody and their faces take on an expression of awe, only reserved for the top end of deep and meaningful artists, who have something profound to say about the human condition. It all started when she warbled her wide-ranging vocals round a cute little number about a moorland house in West Yorkshire.

Kate did release 25 singles in her career, two got to No. 1, of which the second was rather late. "Running Up That Hill" originally from 1984 was rereleased in 2022 as a tie in with the Netflix series "Stranger Things". This got to the top on 17ᵗʰ June that year, a mere 38 years after release and 44 years after her first No. 1, a record for the charts. She was 63 years old when this happened, but only 19 when "Wuthering Heights" became her No. 1 in March 1978.

Wuthering Heights, the novel, came out in 1847 written by Emily Brontë and was an everyday tale of two lovers, Catherine Earnshaw and Heathcliff, whose passionate but troubled relationship is the centrepiece of the book. It was a dark tale of gender inequality, class issues, jealousy and a doomed pairing, where Catherine dies in childbirth at the end of the book. It might just be a good idea if Catherine could come back to see Heathcliff to talk some more about what went wrong but as she is dead this could be an issue here. Unless she could come back as a ghost cunningly disguised as just "Cathy". So that is what Kate Bush did in her famous song.

In the lyrics, three-syllabled Catherine is too long for the lines, so became two-syllabled Cathy. In the song she chats and implores to Heathcliff, saying where did it all go wrong, standing outside his window, while in the throes of hypothermia. Wuthering Heights House on the moors near Haworth in West Yorkshire is rather known for its inclement weather. The tale is a sort of inverse Romeo and Juliet, rather Juliet and Romeo or in this case Cathy and Heathcliff, with the girl instead of the man outside the window. The situation is not resolved by the end of the song. Poor young Cathy is still outside in the cold, notwithstanding that a proper ethereal ghost would not be affected too much by the weather. However, to be serious Kate does do great storytelling lyrics. No one before or since has done "Wuthering Heights" in song, very much a literary first for a No. 1 pop single.

The music is led by Kate's piano and her soaring vocal, with a great hook on the chorus. It is such a catchy melody with a great "eureka" musical moment at 2:36 minutes into the single, where the chorus comes back in to be repeated, with Ian Bairnson's brilliant overlapping guitar solo. This solo could be perhaps just a bit louder in the mix, as Ian has indicated in interviews. The lyrics and music combine to produce a song of deserving unique universality that the record buying public could relate to and buy in droves.

Unusually, there were two music videos made for the song, a white dress Kate Bush filmed singing and dancing indoors, the most commonly shown one, while the second was red dress Kate singing and dancing outdoors on Salisbury Plain, substituting for the West Yorkshire Moors. Otherwise, the films are very similar.

By 1978 I was at university and very much into punk or new wave bands such as the Police, Dire Straits or Talking Heads. Chart singles of a soppy, lovey-dovey persuasion were a definite no-no for me then. However, rather like my secret ABBA liking, the same could be said for Kate Bush and "Wuthering Heights". I will admit now, all these years later, as I did in the previous chapter, for having a Kate Bush crush. She was 19; I was 23, I think we would have made a lovely couple and lived happily... never after. I was skinny, silly, irritating and a bit of a pl***** at that time and Kate had a great escape. Anyway, I digress. "Wuthering Heights" was good. Eventually I acquired Kate's first album A Kick Inside. I also liked "Them Heavy People" and the rocker "James and the Cold Gun" from that.

"Wuthering Heights" was the first No. 1 to be both written and sung by a female artist and in 2020 was voted the 14th best chart No. 1 of all time by The Guardian. Kate Bush, of course, went on to further fame and fortune over the years. I have a copy of her 2011 album, 50 Words for Snow, which has fellow national treasure Stephen Fry narrating different words for snow on the title track. I love the album and more recently she was indicted into the Rock & Roll Hall of Fame in 2023. Finally, for any aliens out there who would like to discover the wonderful, magnificently unique Kate Bush, just latch on to the asteroid named after her in 1998 and press play.

Chapter 16

Video Killed the Radio Star: Buggles

Released 7 September 1979
No. 1 for 1 week
20 October '79
Sales UK: 600,000

Buggles were named after insect bugs supposedly in the same way the Beatles were named after beetles, who of course in turn were influenced in name by the Crickets, Buddy Holly's backing band in the late 1950s. In 1977, when Buggles formed, the trend was to pick a ghastly name for a new band to be a shock horror punk move as in the Damned or Sex Pistols for example. Founder members Trevor Horn, Geoff Downes and Bruce Woolley chose Buggles as an antidote to this pursuit of fake nastiness. The name suggests, in a good sense, classic pop to me and that's just what we got with "Video Killed the Radio Star".

The three main men worked up "Video" in 1979. Bruce wrote most of it and then promptly left the band to form Bruce Woolley and the Camera Club and then put their own version out. This is a frantic, faster, bouncier effort without much in the way of female vocals, almost punk in arrangement. Interesting, but not a patch on the Buggles offering.

That version is altogether more stately, considered and slower, apparently at a 132 beats per minute and in D flat major for those musos amongst you. It took three months to record and contained all the usual rock instrumentation but lots of classical keyboard touches from Geoff. Although Trevor Horn never considered himself a great vocalist, his singing voice sounds perfect for this song and the female vocals by Debi Doss and Linda Jardim-Allen really elevate the song above the Camera Club version.

Lyrically the song looks at how new technology is changing the way music is channelled for the listener and soon to be viewer. This was 1979 and now in 2024 it would have to be retitled "Artificial Intelligence Killed the Video Star." However, back then, the new TV station MTV, which opened at 12.01am on 1st of August 1981, could only play one song video to start off the new channel, which was "Video Killed the Radio Star", you have guessed it.

My own view is that I really like this song. It twists and turns a bit, is very sing-along, has a great melody and is immaculately produced. A lot of the No. 1 songs so far have just got great melodies, which are universally proclaimed, and this is no exception. These are melodies that with little prompting can be remembered years later from a great chart topper. The aforementioned video was simple and effective, filmed in one afternoon and showcases the song really well and is still living happily ever after on MTV even now.

That was the hit for Buggles, so they are more or less one hit wonders. It was not that Trevor and Geoff were not exceptionally talented, but they were rather overtaken by events. I was a prog rock fan in 1980 and was very disappointed to learn that Jon Anderson and Rick Wakeman had left supergroup proggers Yes, leaving them short of a vocalist and keyboard player. Buggles were recording in an adjacent studio to what was left of Yes and they got to know each other and Buggles impressed and were therefore subsumed into Yes. Maybe the rest of Yes should have joined Buggles, but then the affirmative group had long playing seniority. I was very surprised when Trevor and Geoff joined Yes to replace Jon and Rick to record and perform live an album called Drama. It never really worked out for Trevor; he struggled to reach the high parts that only Jon Anderson could do in Yes songs. Yes tried hard with the new arrangement but eventually finished for a while in late 1980. Geoff then joined super group Asia, but Trevor tried something else and hit the big time!

By 2024 Trevor Horn has become one of the most successful producers of all time. Yes, when reformed, Frankie Goes to Hollywood, Grace Jones, the Pet Shop Boys and Robbie Williams, amongst many others have all been his clients. On occasions he has played live as a bass player and singer and redone "Video" to great applause.

Geoff Downes has continued on his merry prog rock way, as a Rick Wakeman-like keyboard player, mainly with versions of Yes or Asia. In an alternative chart universe, it is worth thinking just what would have happened if Trevor and Geoff never joined Yes in 1980. That group may well have split for good, but our dynamic duo could have dominated the '80s as a pop supergroup. Another of those fork in the road, what if moments… but we shall never know.

Chapter 17

There's No One Quite Like Grandma: St. Winifred's School Choir

Released November 1980
No. 1 for 2 weeks
27 December '80 to 5 January '81
Sales UK: 1m

Well, this is a strange one. A year earlier over Christmas 1979 another school choir had a No. 1 in assisting Pink Floyd get to the top with "Another Brick in the Wall". A song with biting, angry, rebellious lyrics about education, which made Alice Cooper's No. 1 "School's Out" from the early '70s look lightweight (more on this in Chapter 44). A year later our featured single could have been born in another universe, never mind on another planet, to illustrate how truly bizarre the UK singles charts were. A song that was light, soppily sentimental, twee beyond belief, with another school children's choir and detested by cool dudes everywhere, had got to No. 1. Yet it sold zillions. It became the companion spouse song to Clive Dunn's Grandad from 1971 (See Chapter 8).

The St. Winifred's School Choir was based at the St. Winifred's Roman Catholic Primary School in Stockport, Greater Manchester forming in 1968 with naturally a shifting cast of singers, as they moved through the age range on to secondary school. The main instigator was a Miss Terri Foley who played the guitar and in the early days a Miss Olive Moore, who conducted the choir. In 1978 the choir were unaccredited backing vocalists on the single "Matchstick Men and Matchstick Cats and Dogs" by Brian and Michael, about paintings by L S Lowry. Unaccredited they might have been, but they got to travel to London for TOTP which must have been very exciting for 8-year-olds. By 1980 the children demanded a headlining role and refused to do schoolwork till Terri Foley, who now also conducted, gave them their own single in their name. This is maybe a slight overstatement here. They were certainly not like those nasty vicious kids who had shouted on the Pink Floyd song a year earlier.

In my own childhood I remember my maternal grandmother best. She was always Granny Wright to me but as a young child I found her a bit scary. In 1971 I was 15, at home playing a Deep Purple song called "Child in Time" where singer Ian Gillan falsetto screams in tune through the song along with some rampant guitar. It is very heavy! Visiting granny did not approve and told me in no uncertain terms to turn it off. I did; she was no fan of that loud obnoxious rock music. I still found her quite terrifying, even as a teenager. She was ok really, and she lived to the grand age of 95. There was no one quite like my grandma but I certainly was not going to write a song about her or her kind, but songwriter Gordon Lorenz had other ideas. The Queen Mother, royal granny, was just the sort of friendly family grandma he had in mind. He had intended to put the song out in August to celebrate her 80th birthday but then decided to hold it back for the Christmas market for grandmas everywhere.

It got to No. 1 just after Christmas replacing "(Just Like) Starting Over" by John Lennon and had been a big seller in the run up to the festivities. It managed one week at No. 1 in the last week in 1980 and repeated that in the first week of January '81. It still sold over a million in 1980 alone.

Musically there is not a hint of rock instrumentation. It is orchestrated, with piano leading. The singing is in tune, nursery rhyme-like, which was the desired effect, with just a hint of harmony here and there. The lead girl singer, Dawn Ralph, does a good job on behalf of the choir, despite a slight lisp. On TOTP they all look wonderfully angelic, with hints of smiles, but none of them move, they stand rock still. The lyrics are full of love and adoration for "Grandma".

Having listened to it again it is staggering that it got to No. 1 at all. John Lennon had been shot and killed and the airwaves were full of his songs including "(Just Like) Starting Over" which was deposed by "Grandma" and then the rereleased "Imagine" was delayed in getting to No. 1 by this song in January '81. I cannot really sugar-coat my own views on "Grandma", sad man that I was. I hated it!

However, the record buying public did not and it is worth considering why. By 1980, as throughout the last 16 years covered in the book, the record buying public were a very diverse lot, in terms of ages, social classes and the way they viewed the world. Almost everybody felt they had a stake in the pop charts. Huge numbers were still watching TOTP and being amazed by the diversity of acts. Therefore, there was a market for a cheesy song about grandma just as there was a market for any song for just about anything. After all, everybody has one, a grandma that is. It would also sell well over Christmas as a stocking filler, when the singles market was at its most potent. First, the song was bought by families to give to grandma. Secondly, the song was bought by parents to give to children, who saw their peers on TV and wanted to join in. Also, I am sure that many children wanted to learn the song to sing to their own grandmothers over Christmas. It just went to prove that everything could sell. It was time for another sentimental, slushy gushy song, most definitely. The proof is there, it got to No. 1.

After "Grandma" the choir existed till the '90s, doing bits here and there but, perhaps not surprisingly, they became one hit wonders. The song was re-recorded in 2014 by 14 of the original choir to raise money for Age Concern. Very recognisable on the front row of the choir in the TOTP choir was Sally Lindsay, who went on to fame as an actress in Coronation Street and The Royle Family. Lead singer Dawn Ralph shuns the public eye, refusing any interview requests, and leads a quiet family life.

It became the bestselling single of 1980, and the royalties went to the school and paid for major refurbishment, so that was good. On my own personal list of worst to good No. 1 singles that I may just do in the Outro, it is safe to say this song may not be in my top 1 or even my top 40! It is quite weird and wacky that it got to the "top of the pops", but there is no denying its pulling power as a chart entity and there is somebody out there for whom this is still their favourite all-time song… perhaps?

Chapter 18

Tainted Love: Soft Cell

Released July 1981
No. 1 for 2 weeks
5 September to 12 September '81
Sales UK: 1.05m

In February 1982 I remember being very impressed by the Soft Cell single "Say Hello, Wave Goodbye". I loved the rich synthesiser sounds, the catchy melody and the doomy break up lyrics. Songs with sad words and a cheerful sing-along tune always seems to work well. Another example would be "Help" by the Beatles, where John Lennon's pleading lyrics were put over an uplifting tune. Marc Almond's vocals just soar with an air of pathos and melancholy, over an orchestral luscious melody, just the perfect pop single for breaking up to. However, it only got to No. 3 and therefore cannot have star billing in this chapter. Just why was "Tainted Love" by Soft Cell, six months earlier, even more popular as a No. 1? Time to try and find out.

Soft Cell were a typical early '80s new romantic synth duo with Marc Almond on vocals and David Ball on everything else. They had recorded an album called Non-Stop Erotic Cabaret which dealt with suitable "rock'n'roll synth" topics such as sleaze and squalor, being very much a more "entertaining" antidote perhaps to the previous year's "Grandma" epic. "Tainted Love", "Touch" and "Say Hello, Wave Goodbye" all came from the album in that order as singles. If "Hello" had come out before the other two maybe it would have got to No. 1, while "Tainted", if it had come out last would only have got to No. 3? Or maybe not, another hypothetical what if moment, the charts, like life, were full of them.

"Tainted" had an interesting history. The song has connections to the USA, T. Rex, Wigan and Marilyn Manson and was therefore a song with transatlantic geographical links. It started in 1964, when the song was written by a chap called Ed Cobb of the Four Preps group in the USA. It was given to a soul singer, Gloria Jones, to sing. It failed to chart and was put to bed for a while. Meanwhile, some years later Gloria became the partner of Marc Bolan of T. Rex and sadly was driving the car that crashed and killed Marc in 1977, referred to in the "Telegram Sam" chapter (9) in the book. Meanwhile, in 1973 Northern Soul Club DJ Richard Searling was in the USA and picked up a copy of Gloria's "Tainted" and brought it back over here to play "up north" in clubs in places such as Wigan and Bolton. I was vaguely aware of Northern Soul. It travelled as far south as Nottingham, where I was still living in 1973 and seemed to have consisted of all-nighters. It was danced by very tough looking skinhead men, yet without a hint of "bovver" with everybody being very happy to leave the clubs at dawn and go on to have a full English breakfast on a Sunday morning. "Tainted" as a song was well known therefore and came to the attention of Marc and David.

The Soft Cell version was recorded in a mere half a day and was a first take on the vocal by Marc. It became the 2nd biggest selling single of '81 after "Don't You Want Me" by the Human League.

Musically the track seems to me to be cyclical, and every one circuit or 8th beat there is an extra "duh duh" synth drum sound that gives the song its distinctive hook. A very non-technical explanation of saying just how memorable and classy the tune is to me. Marc's clear and timed to perfection vocal lines just add even more '80s gloss to the song.

Lyrically the words tell of a love that is not right, tainted, of someone who needs to pull out of the relationship. Should that someone stay or go? In the end the person stays being sexually addicted… perhaps. The lyrics appear straightforward but there is possibly just an element of vagueness there. Anyway, the relationship appears not to end. "Tainted Love

Two" should have been a follow up single to resolve the matter. The video is even more enigmatic, where David Ball as a cricketer meets Marc Almond dressed in a toga just to confuse us all more. "Tainted Toga Love" could have been a 3rd single to make a trilogy, and then would come the book, the film etc? I will stop there.

It was a huge seller in the UK, despite only being at No. 1 for two weeks. In the USA the single got to No. 8 but stayed in the Billboard Charts for 43 weeks, which is a record.

I liked the song and can appreciate why the public really loved it too. It has a cheerful tune, great melody, well-sung, musical hooks and slightly enigmatic lyrics, all done and dusted in only 2:41 minutes. It has a sexy, sleazy feel and was very much in tune with the new romantic fashion of the time.

There was a version of "Tainted" by American, shock gothic rock person, Marilyn Manson from 2001. This is more grungy aurally and the video is a sleaze orientated, big time epic and not for the sexually inhibited. Personally, I would stick with Soft Cell.

After "Tainted" Soft Cell soon had a No. 2 hit with "Touch", then "Hello" got to No. 3. They split in 1984, reformed in 2001 and have then got together sporadically since. Marc Almond has had a successful and prolific solo career putting out over 20 albums of his own. He has finally admitted in the last few years, that he grew up listening to '70s classic rock and will often guest live with prog rock dinosaurs Jethro Tull for their Christmas shows. Marc was really just an old hippy all along, just in disguise.

It could be argued that by '81 the charts had returned to normal, as our song was fundamentally about sex, rather than an elderly much loved family member. But then there was still no "normal" about chart content. Anything about everything could still be a hit, which might just lead us in to one of the most wonderfully annoying No. 1s of all time for '82, especially if you had the misfortune to be called Eileen!

Chapter 19

Come On Eileen: Dexys Midnight Runners

Released 25 June 1982
No. 1 for 4 weeks
7 August to 28 August '82
Sales UK: 1.33m

In my village table tennis club, we have a very nice elderly lady called "guess what", who has to respond to the vaguely in tune exhortation of "Come On Eileen" when it is her turn to play. It might be me that does this; it may be others; I can't say to protect the guilty. The rumour is that this is a line from a pop song from 42 years ago, which is still part of the collective consciousness of the nation, especially if you are getting on a bit. It was probably a great song, unless you had the misfortune to be actually called Eileen and were around to be sung at incessantly in 1982. In 2024 only one baby girl in 4000 is called Eileen in the UK, a name on the decline and I blame our featured song!

Meanwhile Dexys Midnight Runners were a Birmingham soul group, who came about in the late 1970s. They were coolly or strangely named after a recreational drug called Dexedrine; a type of amphetamine used to keep the dancers going till breakfast in Northern Soul clubs. Dexys had a No. 1 hit with "Geno" in 1980 but by 1982 were down on their luck with not much happening. They needed a biggie, and they got one! This year an album was put out called Too-Rye-Ay and they changed their dress code to dungarees, scarves and leather waistcoats to give them an Irish gypsy look. Main man Kevin Rowland got together with fellow band members Jim Paterson and Billy Adams to write "Come On Eileen". It turned out eventually that most of the song had been written by recently departed band member Kevin Archer, who only belatedly, some years later, got his royalties.

It was a summer No. 1 hit in the UK over August, with huge sales, eventually becoming the biggest seller of 1982. In 2015 it was voted in an ITV poll the 6th best No. 1 of the '80s and won the '82 Brit award for Best Single. In the USA it was not No. 1 till April 1983, where it displaced "Billie Jean" by Michael Jackson (featured in the next chapter). You could say "Eileen" did rather well.

Musically it features banjo, accordion, fiddle and saxophone. It is an upbeat, simple tune, where the sing-along memorable chorus (one perhaps unfortunately you can never forget, even 40 years later) uplifts the whole song to a level above the verses like a good pop song should. Perhaps its absolute unique selling point is the long fade out where it speeds up! It starts off at 102 beats per minute (bpm) and finishes at 116 bpm. This is the bit at karaoke or discos where everybody including me but only once that I will admit to, starts singing and leaping in the air then collapsing in a drunken "nice to get to know you" heap at the end. I wonder how many injuries and pulled muscles there have been at the climax of this song. As well as universally irritating all Eileens everywhere, it is an injury prone song. It has a lot to answer for!

Lyrically it is almost too much, having 70 plus short lines of words including lots of the famous "too-ra-loo-ra, too-ra-loo-rye" bits but the best line is No. 37 which says "take off everything" as in clothes because "Eileen" is actually about unrequited sex, just when you thought it was a very lovey-dovey sing-along. Kevin Rowland enjoyed a frustrating adolescence at school, unable to get it together with girls, so he wrote a song about it. "Eileen" may or may not have been a real girl. In any case, 4 minutes plus of frantic singing and dancing to the song would have left Kevin and Eileen or anyone else, incapable of much further action at all, at the song's conclusion. Best not to think too much about the lyrics and just dance. Do lyrics actually matter in a song like this? The music itself is so overpowering, it is a very difficult track to sit still to, even for a cool dude like me.

It is pretty easy to see and hear why this was a No. 1 for all the reasons mentioned so far. Uplifting, good fun, danceable, sing-along, great for drunks everywhere and just oh so memorable, probably for all eternity. I hated it, just because I can never forget it. Having listened to it again about 24 hours ago, after a gap of 40 years, I am having "Eileen" nightmares all over again.

After "Eileen" Dexys had 1 more big hit, a cover of Van Morrison's "Jackie Wilson Said (I'm in Heaven When You Smile)" which got to No. 5 in October '82. On TOTP a background picture was put up of Jackie Wilson the '60s soul singer, subject of the song, when the band performed. However, the picture was actually of Jocky Wilson the darts player. Deliberate or accidental, it promoted more sales of the single. Dexys split in '87 but like other bands singled out in this book, they then reformed, broke up, reformed again, etc. There was still a version featuring Kevin Rowland as the main man in 2023. At the last count there had been over 50 band members, including Kevin of course, but it is also worth mentioning Helen O'Hara who was the energetic fiddle player on "Eileen".

So in summary I recognise "Come on Eileen" as a great pop single. It had and still has 40 years later, universal appeal being memorable and simply unforgettable. For me, perhaps I need a huge amount of alcohol to get the tune out of my head before the next chapter. Oh dear, it did not work… "Come on Eileen"!

Chapter 20

Billie Jean: Michael Jackson

Released 2nd January 1983
No. 1 for 1 week
5 March '83
Sales UK: 500,000

It is amazing that a song so universally well-known and acclaimed was only No. 1 for one week. "Too Shy" by Kajagoogoo and "Total Eclipse of the Heart" by Bonnie Tyler were the either side No. 1s, fine records but hardly of the earth-shattering cultural and musical significance which "Billie Jean" had. Thriller, now the best-selling album of all time had been released in 1982 and maybe people had bought that as the parent album of "Billie" and already had the song there. Elsewhere in the world "Billie" was a massive mega best seller and Michael Jackson would hardly be pleading poverty.

Throughout the '70s I was always aware of Michael Jackson (M J) as child star, then teenage sensation. He was the 8th child of a very large family, who by 1979 as a young adult had put his first major album out, Off the Wall with its attendant major single "Don't Stop 'Til You Get Enough", which got to No. 3. He was all right with me as I much preferred the Jackson 5 to the Osmonds and I much preferred Michael to Donny, for what it was worth. He was not quite yet the "King of Pop" and the global phenomenon in song, dance and fashion he was to become. That was all to change with the album Thriller, released toward the end of 1982.

This spawned three biggies. "Thriller", the single written by Brit, Rod Temperton, once of the band Heatwave, which seemed to last forever with its super expensive video. Next was "Beat It" (my favourite of the three) with the amazing Eddie Van Halen tapping guitar solo for metalheads everywhere and then

"Billie Jean" which was definitely not a song about the tennis player.

Musically just where to begin? The throbbing, gyrating, wonderful bass does it for me played by Louis Johnson and then being overlain by synthesised keyboards, which are not overplayed. There is no wall of sound here; you can hear virtually every instrument where the economy and tightness of the players just adds to the funkiness of the track. M J's vocals were recorded in one take and are quite low for his normal singing register. The song moves along at 117 bpm and never wavers, which just gives it that amazing dance groove.

Lyrically it is a song about groupies and Michael definitely wants you to know Billie Jean was not his lover and he is not the father of any disputed child, despite what Billie Jean says. The Jackson 5 were pursued by women in the '70s and the stereotypical groupies were putting in shifts with our family of brothers. I always thought groupies used all their energy lusting after rock groups like Led Zeppelin. M J had been accused already of fathering twins, so the lyrics were vaguely autographical for him to deny. It was thought best to get these denials in now in song, before anything went to court.

The video was the first by a black artist to be played in heavy rotation by MTV. It features M J in a satin suit, red tie and white shirt, which became the look across the USA in '83. Michael dances his way through the film and cannot really resist the allure of Billy Jean, as he approaches her hotel room at the end of the song. But it was a live performance of the song, which was going to send it across this universe and into the next.

M J was to appear performing "Billie" at the Motown 25 Years Special TV show and really wanted to do something different, and that he did. Despite the best part of 40 years of practising the Moonwalk, I still encourage a hernia every time I try but M J perfected this perfectly on this show, while wearing one white glove, which became another trademark. If you watch the video, I still cannot fathom out what he is doing with his sliding feet or is it a sliding floor? This became an iconic historical "rock'n'pop" moment in action.

Needless to say, at the time and over the years, the awards have flown in for the song. BBC Radio 2 has voted "Billie" the best dance track of all time and in numerous polls of best single of all time, it also scores very highly. Funnily enough, I still prefer "Beat It" because of the rock feel and aforementioned guitar solo. I would put "Billie" ahead of "Thriller" though in my preferences. The killer punch for me about "Billie" is just that incredible groove, that M J just had that knack and feel for.

This is an obvious No. 1 not just for all the attributes mentioned, but for the momentum to superstardom of M J, so by 1982/3 he could do no wrong. He became the "King of Pop" and more or less retained that status till he died. Bizarrely, because let's face it he did not need the money; he used "Billie" in a commercial for Pepsi-Cola a few years later. Even more super bizarrely, a stray firework went off during the film being made, badly burning M J's hair. Perhaps this was a sign of things to come, where misfortune was to befall him eventually. After Thriller, though he did have two more mega magnificent albums, Bad in '87 and Dangerous in '91, with all their attendant singles. Eventually he was able to accumulate 15 Grammys and six Brit awards.

By the noughties, all was not well in the Jackson universe. His skin colour seemed to be getting lighter, which may or may not have been natural progression. But more serious were sexual allegations regarding children. This was fuelled by rumour, counter rumour and out of court settlements and his reputation took quite a beating. If he had lived, maybe more of this would have come out. Michael Jackson was to die on 25 June 2009 of a cardiac arrest from an overdose of sedatives and propofol. His doctor Conrad Murray was convicted of involuntary manslaughter.

Michael Jackson was only 50. It was quite a shock; I remember feeling the same when Prince died in April 2016. His legacy in terms of music and culture is enormous. His "Billie Jean" was just wonderful and epic but that is not quite the end of the story.

Most covers of most songs add nothing new and are poor reinterpretations, but rock singer Chris Cornell's version of "Billie Jean" is something else. It comes over as a bluesy, sleazy rock song with great singing and a stunning guitar solo. I love it, but I would suspect most punters who bought the original would not. For all his faults, I still think Michael would have approved though.

Chapter 21

Do They Know It's Christmas?: Band Aid

Released 3rd December 1984
No. 1 for 5 weeks
15 December '84 to 12 January '85
Sales UK: 3m

This is the second biggest selling single of all time, which eventually raised £8m for famine relief in Ethiopia. It is a super famous record, which will be known forever. Was it any good? Well, I think it was, although as cowriter Midge Ure has hinted, that did not really matter. It was really all about the money and the good charitable cause it went to. It was called Band Aid, as a pop band was going to make the single and a "band aid plaster" could represent healing to make the famine "go away". So, it started as a song at first, which had no group or singer, as it was just really a concept that needed to be made into a musical reality. The song itself "Do They Know It's Christmas?" has now been released four times in different anniversary versions for slightly different causes. As I write in early 2024 it is coming up to its 40th birthday, so I wonder if we may see some further action on this later in the year?

    This is a rough timeline as to what happened back in '84. A young, highly successful couple were watching the BBC News on 23rd October 1984, as you do and reporter Michael Buerk came on and produced a film about a famine in Ethiopia, as the rains had failed. Relief agencies could not get food out quick enough; people, and especially children, were dying. It was a harrowing film, quite stark and brutal and very upsetting for the watching Bob Geldof (Boomtown Rats) and Paula Yates (TV presenter). They watched and then worked out a way they thought they could make a difference. Let's make a charity single, get anybody who is anybody on it and release it very quickly in time for Christmas. That is exactly what happened. Concept to reality in less than two months!

    First Bob met Midge Ure of Ultravox, who agreed to write some suitable music, melody and a backing track, to fit in with Bob's lyrics for "Do They Know It's Christmas?" Meanwhile, Paula Yates contacted the top pop stars to come and sing on the record. She had interviewed and flirted with most of them, while co-hosting The Tube TV show with co-presenter Jools Holland. The backing track was worked up by John Taylor: bass and Andy Taylor: guitar (no relation to each other or the author) both of Duran Duran. Midge was able to provide keyboards and programming including synth drums. Phil Collins was to add real drums on the big day.

    The big day was 25th November, starting with all attendees on the chorus and then with individuals adding their singing bits afterwards. In order, this was Paul Young, deputising for unavailable David Bowie, Boy George flown in on Concorde from America especially, George Michael, Simon Le Bon (Duran Duran), Tony Hadley (Spandau Ballet) and Bono. Sting flitted in and out adding harmonies with the lead singers. Loads of other people turned up to help on the chorus but probably the most popular attendees were Francis Rossi and Rick Parfitt of Status Quo, who allegedly supplied the drugs, being too hung over from the night before to make any meaningful contribution to the music on the day. It was good to know the spirit (or the spliff) of "rock'n'roll" was alive and well in this venture, along with its worthy cause. Non-attendees Paul McCartney and David Bowie left supportive messages on the B side of "Christmas".

    The single of "Christmas" was rushed out on the 3rd of December '84 and got to No. 1 on the 15th of December, staying there for five weeks and selling a monster mega 3m copies over that period. It has gone on to be released in various forms three more times, till now.

Band Aid II (maybe to be a bit "arty" here, Roman numerals were used instead of No. 2) came out in 1989 and was arranged by Stock, Aitken and Waterman, the hot production team of the time. It spent three weeks at No. 1 over December '89. Band Aid 20 came out in 2004 on the 20th anniversary, this time spending four weeks at No. 1. Monies collected went to famine relief in both these cases. However, Band Aid 30 out in 2014 collected money to help fight an Ebola outbreak in Africa. It remains to be seen whether Band Aid 40 will be out later this year?

It is very obvious perhaps why this song was a hit. I actually liked the tune and lyrics, thought they had merit on their own, even without the charitable status of "Christmas" being brought into play. However, the personal drive of Bob, Paula and Midge went a long way to propel it to its eventual zenith as a single of cultural, social and great economic significance. Bob in particular was a force of nature, in steamrolling it all through. It was him who persuaded Prime Minister Margaret Thatcher, of all people, to waive VAT tax on the single, so more profit could go to charity. These were still the days when the charts meant something to millions of people and in this case Band Aid was national news, replacing relationships, football, and politics as the main topic of conversation at work, home, in the pub and out on the street. This all helped sales.

There was, perhaps unfairly, some criticism about Band Aid being self-righteousness. The modern equivalent of this might be phrases like "woke" or "virtue signalling". Left wing political band Chumbawamba put out a single in 1986 called "Pictures of Starving Children Sell Records". It is of course true there was a knock-on effect for the artists in sales, but I feel Bob, Paula and Midge did it totally for altruistic reasons in the right spirit. I think it is super churlish for the single to have any criticism of this nature. It did raise £8m for charity after all, which was the unique selling point of "Christmas", not just its artistic quality. I think we can excuse the massive party that followed on the big day with beer, dope and cocaine just this once, I am sure that was all paid for with all the attendees' own money.

After Band Aid was Live Aid, the famous all day live charity concert for famine relief, in July 1985, which raised even more money, and was a very memorable day. However, as the cliché goes Live Aid is another story for another book. "Christmas" was undeniable, as one the great pop singles of all time because of its wider significance, as a very much unique national event never to be repeated… till 1997 (See Chapter 34). Meanwhile, I am looking forward to Band Aid 500 in 2584, when Bob Geldof will be back in all his grumpy glory, as an avatar hologram asking us to buy again till it hurts!

Chapter 22

19: Paul Hardcastle

Released April 1985
No. 1 for 5 weeks
11 May to 8 June '85
Sales UK: 785,000

In the 1960s and '70s young men from the USA were taken across by plane to fight in the Vietnam war, for a 12-month tour, their average age was 19, compared to 26 for combat troops in WW2. From day one, they were exposed to hostile fire all the time; it was all very stressful, as well as extremely dangerous. Those who made it home were traumatised, finding it difficult to settle down, and were often in trouble with the police, being arrested and put in jail. In WW2 soldiers would travel back to the USA in troopships from Europe, where they could support and help each other over wartime traumas. Coming back from jungle combat in Vietnam, the now 20-year-olds could be returned by plane to the USA in less than 48 hrs. There was no hero's welcome when they arrived, and they were cast adrift to supposedly get on with their lives, with no further support. In reality, many were suffering Post Traumatic Stress Disorder (PTSD) with feelings of rage, alienation or guilt. Why did all this happen and was it worth it? What was it for?

As the last question is left hanging, I have to say the above paragraph is not my words. I have merely expanded slightly on the mainly spoken lyrics, sampled and present on the "19" single. Why is it that this absolutely lyrically remarkable song got to No. 1 in the UK single charts, sometimes populated by chickens (see next year) or combine harvesters (regress to 1976)? However, as I have repeatedly said in this book, any song seemingly at any time of any quality or specific uniqueness can get to No. 1 and this is no exception! Also, serious lyrics were put over a rather cheerful, jaunty, foot-tapping dance number, as happens on "19". It is the sad words, uplifting music paradox again, which does not seem to stop a song being a hit! In this case it could be maybe another record, where the lyrics were devalued by a quaint little tune. In discos and clubs where this was played, how many listened to the lyrics and rather like the Vietnam War, what was it all for? Well maybe the cheerful tune just pulled the punters in to listen to the lyrics a little, to absorb some of the message perhaps. It is time to find out or at least hazard a guess.

Paul Hardcastle was rather a typical early '80s band keyboard player in that he had mastered sequencers, emulators, synthesisers and drum machines. The days of just playing piano and organ were long gone. He had played with a band called Direct Drive, which morphed into a second band First Light. Two bands that got nowhere, so like many before him he was waiting for the big break.

The springboard for "19" was when Paul had watched a 1982 ABC news documentary from America called "Vietnam Requiem" about returning soldiers from the war, who were suffering with PTSD. Much of the narration here was by a Peter Thomas, whose commentary was extensively sampled in "19" to make up most of the lyrics. There was a special stuttering effect to create the musical hook, this being done on an emulator by repeatedly pressing the "ni ni ni" of "nineteen" on the keyboard. This can sound almost comical and, again, did it distract a little from the antiwar sentiment of the song?

No matter, it was the biggest selling UK single of 1985 and was always high up in polls of '80s best singles. It stayed at No. 1 for five weeks. Paul never appeared live on TOTP, as he sent a slightly different video in each week based on images from the "Vietnam Requiem" film he had permission to use. He also created an extended "Destruction" dance mix to play in the clubs. It did not get to No. 1 in the USA but hung around the charts for a long time as a steady seller. There was some feeling from some in the USA that the song was anti-American.

Lyrically the spoken words are some of the most direct, dramatic "in your face" ever. They are very brutal about just what happened to the very young Vietnam vets, home age 20 and severely traumatised. Is this why it got to No. 1 though? I suspect not. As indicated earlier, while not up to the wonderful groove standard of Billie Jean, the instrumental track was great to dance to and the words perhaps would become secondary. Maybe Paul felt to get a message out about Vietnam and be anti-war he needed to produce a "little light music". My favourite anti-war song, as no doubt it will be for many others, is "War" by American Soul singer Edwin Starr, put out in 1970, which was a UK No. 3 (so therefore is banned from being a chapter on its own in this book). My personal view is that "19" is a great single lyrically and a good single instrumentally. Put that together and overall, you had a powerful musical statement of intent, which people bought in droves. While Paul made a few quid for his efforts, I do not doubt his sincerity in wanting to bring the horrors of Vietnam to our attention. No virtue signalling here!

The TOTP new theme tune in 1986 "The Wizard" was by Paul which lasted on the show till 1991 and he has continued to make classy, jazzy, dancey, synthy music ever since, just maybe not quite at the same artistic and commercial level as (Ni Ni Ni Nineteen) "19".

Chapter 23

The Chicken Song: Spitting Image

Released April 1986
No. 1 for 3 weeks
17 May to 31 May '86
Sales UK: 200,000 approx.

A caricature is a drawing of someone, where the obvious features are exaggerated for comic effect. For example, a caricature of the author would elongate the nose, which is rather big in the first place, while shining up his nearly bald scalp to look like a mirror. The whole figure would have a large jumper with matchstick legs to accentuate his essential skinniness. The 1980s prime minister Margaret Thatcher might wear a suit, have an unshaven visage, and smoke a cigar to show her masculine features, in being able to dominate her all male government cabinet. While I can do myself as an original caricature here, Mrs T just might have been done before in a cunning little parody satire TV programme called Spitting Image. You may have heard of it.

Spitting Image started in 1984. It was set up by Martin Lambie-Nairn, on behalf of ITV and used the puppetry genius of Peter Fluck and Roger Law. It turned 2-dimensional caricature drawings into 3D latex puppets and got them to be voiced by actors. It then relied on cutting edge satire scripts to bring the puppets to life. All life was lampooned including politics, entertainment, sport and culture but current politicians and the royal family got the most attention, which did not always go down too well. Most pop stars though loved their puppets, including Phil Collins. Genesis used Spitting Image puppets of themselves for the video to go with "The Land of Confusion" single in November '86. The first episode of Spitting Image attracted many viewers but then tailed off quite quickly.

The puppets were a hit and the voice-over actors including Harry Enfield, Chris Barrie and Steve Nallon as Thatcher were great. However, by late 1985 new writers Rob Grant and Doug Naylor came in and soon up to 15m were watching every week and it was the most popular talked about show on TV, just ripe for an associated single to make lots of money and perhaps have just a smidgeon of (no) artistic credibility in the process. Also, in our mixed up charts and our mixed up book it was about time for another comedy record. The last one was "Combine" ten years ago.

"The Chicken Song" (initially to be called "The Holiday Song") was written musically by Philip Pope, in the style of the classic stupendous Black Lace epics such as "Agadoo" and "Do the Conga". The melody and rhythm were light and bouncy, inoffensive and if blind drunk or perhaps even better aurally drunk, then you could still tap your feet in time. The lyrics were written by Rob and Doug and were utter and total nonsense and they would probably be happy to take that comment as a compliment. It was sung casually and deadpan by Michael Fenton Stevens. Two lines are worth repeating "Hold a chicken in the air, stick a deckchair up your nose". I suspect the second line would like to have had a different last word but taste, decency and especially not wanting to be banned, prevailed. Compromise is the next best thing, when there is money to be made.

Having been released in April '86, it actually got to No. 1 in May, just in time for the holiday season for the masses everywhere to join in and sing along on the beach and down the disco. It got to No. 1 in Ireland, but my extensive research finds it did not chart anywhere else in the world. I just can't think why! This is even though a celebrity mega mix had been released with vocals from "Bob Dylan, Tina Turner and Bruce Springsteen." Not the real ones of course; they were all out to lunch. On TOTP actors dressed up in no doubt very hot latex puppet suits and mimed to the song. It still made no difference, the song still stayed at No. 1 for another two weeks.

This song was of its time and became on obvious hit on the back of the TV series. Would it have been any good as a stand-alone single? Probably not, it would have had no context. Some have argued with only the slightest of smirks, that this song was put out to test just how gullible and stupid the buying public could be. We made it, you bought it, and the joke is on you. On the other hand, it was a fun single, gave joy to millions and comedy, even when it is totally ridiculous, is a great antidote to the traumas of everyday life, especially in the mid-80s. It has been 10 long years in the book since our last comedy record ("Combine") and of course we need a break from singles that changed history or had a serious frowny face with grim lyrics. Personally, I really, really… hated it passionately, especially when I heard it again after 38 years! I had also totally forgotten it to preserve my mental health. Every single so far from '64 to '85 had some residual memory for me but not this one. I can though (just about) understand why it was a hit.

Spitting Image spluttered on into the '90s. It was still very funny at times, but like other musical and cultural interludes in the book, eventually had its day, finishing in 1996. Many of the puppets were sold at Sotheby's a few years later and original puppet maker Roger Law donated all his spitting image artefacts to Cambridge University in 2018 to be saved for posterity for the nation. There was an attempt to bring back Spitting Image to BritBox pay per view TV in 2020 but it never really took off. Meanwhile, there is still someone somewhere stuck in a time warp on holiday trying to "Hold a chicken in the air" and "stick a deckchair up your… nose"!

Chapter 24

It's a Sin: Pet Shop Boys

Released 15 June 1987
No. 1 for 3 weeks
4 July to 18 July '87
Sales UK: 500,000

Two people bands had really taken off in the '80s. The conventional rock or pop band in the '70s was drums, bass guitar, lead guitar, singer, and with keyboards that were normally just piano and organ. However, this was to change with new technology. During this time and then evolving into the '80s was the rise of the synthesiser to produce any music, be it a single note or wall of sound that you wanted. It could be programmed to produce repeated sounds rhythmically, thus becoming a drum machine and the "synth" became associated with the then modern terms like sequencer and emulator. They dominated pop music in the '80s and suddenly you could dispense with the drums, bass and guitar and still get that funky dance groove you wanted. All this with polyphonic multiple melody lines all programmed into a minute keyboard, half the size of a piano.

Hence the rise of the two people band, one to sing, the second to stand there, looking wise, intellectual and cool, while looking at an automated keyboard and pressing the odd note periodically. We have seen this from Soft Cell in '81 but the Pet Shop Boys took this to another level, where in addition to having this new technology, they were able to persistently write tunes with great melodies and wonderful musical hooks over the years. Despite the lack of conventional rock instrumentation, I rather liked them but in order to be cool, rather with my liking for ABBA, I kept my Pet Shop Boys ardour quiet at the time.

The Pet Shop Boys were formed in 1981 consisting of Neil Tennant on vocals and Chris Lowe on being the quiet one and multiple keyboards. By 2024 they have 22 top 10 hits, 4 UK No. 1s and have sold 50m singles and albums worldwide, so they are not strapped for cash on a night out. Yet the first few years were a struggle. Neil Tennant continued to work as a reporter and then deputy editor for Smash Hits magazine until April '85. The breakthrough was "West End Girls" in late '85, which became their first No. 1. I really liked this, thinking the instrumentation was so cool and smooth. It was very much of the moment but is still played on the radio today. Unlike some: "Combine" from '76 and "Chicken" from '86, both featured in this book are just some past No. 1s not to be heard on the radio now. However, the Pet Shop Boys have never gone away, their tunes are just so memorable. Through '86 they had more hits including "Opportunities (Let's Make Lots of Money)" and "Suburbia" and they then came up with their second No. 1 from a sense of guilt that the writer was a sinner! A confessional song and it made great pop music.

I went to a Roman Catholic boys grammar school. It was brilliant, especially the sport, it got me to university and gave me, I hope, a great moral code and a good sense of right and wrong. However, it did give me a feeling at times that everything I did was wrong. I could never be quite good enough. I always had a sense of shame. I did as a teenager go to confession once every three weeks to repent my sins and ask, "Father forgive me." Neil Tennant could have written "It's a Sin" just for me with those lyrics, but then he too went to a Roman Catholic school and felt the same way. The difference was I was totally talentless as a musician and could not have written a mega selling song about it. Neil's lyrics totally reflect my own experience as a teenager. This is also yet another song suffering or benefiting from the sad lyrics, cheerful tune paradox.

Musically the track is grandiose and majestic. There are drum rolls, thunderclaps, with massive "synth" string chordal progressions and at the root of it all, a great melody to sing along to. Neil's voice just has an air of sadness and vulnerability that adds more charm. The video shows Neil looking guilty for everything. Chris as his jailer and, bizarrely, actor Ron Moody as his judge are present in a gothic dry ice setting that might be hell or, if you get time off for good behaviour as a Catholic, could be purgatory.

There was a great cover of this song at the 2021 Brit awards by Elton John and singer Olly Alexander of the Years & Years band. Elton, as he does, plays a great bit of tinkling piano in the intro and outro and does some singing, but the brilliant vocals of Olly add even more pathos and sadness to the track. The bit in the middle of course, being the Brits, was completely overblown having mass dancers and singers on a set the size of a small planet and a lighting electricity bill that would bankrupt most countries. They should have left it as just Elton and Olly as the only singers. The starkness of that production would have brought out the essential melancholy of the song even more.

For the next 37 years the Pet Shop Boys have never gone away, having had hit after hit. The two further No. 1s were "Always on My Mind" in late '87 and "Heart" early in the following year. They have deservingly won numerous awards, perhaps the best (or not) was the New Musical Express (NME) Godlike Genius award in 2017. "It's a Sin" is a great pop song up there with the best of them. I think maybe Neil Tennant, when you and Chris can write songs like this, that you have definitely been forgiven, and you should have no shame. Just remember you brought pleasure to millions with a wonderful song! (I did not buy it at the time, such shame. "Neil forgive me").

Chapter 25

He Ain't Heavy, He's My Brother: The Hollies

Re-release August 1988
No. 1 for 2 weeks
24 September to 1 October '88
Sales UK: 500,000

In 1884 in "The Parables of Jesus", James Wells, Moderator of the United Free Church of Scotland recorded that someone had come across a little girl carrying a young boy of equal weight on her back. When she was asked was that not heavy and hard work, she replied, "He ain't heavy, he's my brother," showing a wonderful sibling generosity of spirit and selflessness. This is the first occasion where the now well-known saying was probably used. Some years later in 1918 Father Edward Flanagan saw a similar act, as a young boy was carrying another young boy stricken with polio and he made the same reply when asked the same question. This was at the Boys Town children's home in the USA. By the 1940s Father Flanagan saw similar comments in a magazine about a boy carrying another boy on his back as a selfless act and he also said "He ain't heavy, he's my brother." The "brother" phrase then subsequently became adopted as the motto or slogan for the Boys Home. Both accounts show a very worthy act of the best that humans can do. It provided an altruistic act of high moral intent, that one day could just be used for a promising, uplifting song title.

Meanwhile, back in the land of pop stars and pop charts in late 1988, Elton John, courtesy of a lager advert, was about to get a No. 1 hit record but only as a piano player. I am sure Elton and his accountant realised the significance of extra money coming in then, although the record buying public possibly did not know he was the piano player on a September No. 1. In 1969 he had played piano as a session musician, known then as Reg

Dwight, his original name, for the Hollies on their original release of "Brother", the song then getting to No. 3. On rerelease in 1988, on the back of the song being currently used in a Miller Lite beer advert, it got to No. 1 for two weeks in late September/very early October.

So "Brother" had a quite amazing back story and an equally amazing front story as there are several other versions of the song. It was written by Bobby Scott and Bob Russell in the late '60s. Sadly, during the writing period Bob was dying of Lymphoma but it is to his great credit he was able to help complete "Brother" before he died. The first version of the song in early '69 was put out by Kelly Gordon, but the first significant chart action was by the Hollies version in late '69, when it had got nearly to the top, stalling at No. 3.

The Hollies had been formed in 1962 by childhood friends Allan Clarke and Graham Nash from Manchester. They were naturally able to sing great harmonies together with Graham taking the top line and this became their early trademark in hits like "I'm Alive", a No. 1 in 1965 and "Stop Stop Stop", which got to No. 2 in 1966. Graham Nash left the band in 1968 to go and be part of a transatlantic supergroup, Crosby, Stills, Nash and Young. This left a core of Allan Clarke, Tony Hicks, Bobby Elliott and Nash replacement Terry Sylvester to record "Brother", with the help of our Reg, who was only to become legally name changed to Elton Hercules John in 1972.

The lyrics are simple, have universality about them, in giving help and support to someone less fortunate than themselves. There was no hint of irony, and none was needed for these heartfelt words, which just sum up the best of the human condition. The song is definitely very much a tearjerker.

The music does back that up. A very plaintive harmonica gets the track going with luscious strings behind, leaving Allan Clarke's pitch perfect voice to dominate the song, with some nice harmonies from the others on the chorusy bits.

So, after initially peaking at No. 3 in '69 and then being released 19 years later, it got to No. 1. But then great songs are timeless across the years. This is a song that is still celebrated today, by repeated plays on any radio station across the land. Like some more of the better songs on my list, lyrics and tune are so memorable that they become unforgettable and part of the collective consciousness of the nation. It is not surprising it got to No. 1 eventually. A sentiment about helping others by some hard physical effort from somebody else is a lyric that we can all relate to. Also, beyond the physical it could mean he's no trouble and I will "carry" him, and his problems if necessary, as a token of fraternal love. There is no irony here, this is a song that means it and is all the better for it! With its sad melancholic yet epic feel, it was a tearjerker all the way to the bank.

Other versions include the Justice Collective from 2012, who were raising funds for the relatives of the Hillsborough Disaster, a worthy cause and this got to No. 1 then. There were album versions by Donny Hathaway in 1971 on his self-titled LP and by Olivia Newton-John on her 1975 album "Clearly Love" But it is the twice-released Hollies version that is almost certainly the best and most well-known.

The Hollies have carried on in some form from 1988 all the way to the present day, still singing "Brother" and moving the audience to tears. Personally, it is bit too slushy for me, sad man that I am, but I totally recognise its universal appeal about the very best of the human condition. Now in these troubled times of the mid 2020s, maybe it is time for a re-rerelease of "He Ain't Heavy He's My Brother" to remind us, the human race, of our potential to be wonderfully nice to each other. This new release would be for a suitable charitable cause of course. Even miserable me would buy it!

Chapter 26

Ride on Time: Black Box

Released August 1989
No. 1 for 6 weeks
9 September 9 to 14 October '89
Sales UK: 1.1m

This was a song mired in controversy involving unauthorised sampling, disreputable lip-syncing, lawsuits, regrets and apologies. Apart from that, it actually sounded great, although you could never be quite sure who did what, where and when. It also happened to become the biggest selling single of 1989.

Black Box was a front name for a trio of Italian music producers, who wanted to put out contemporary pop dance music with the power of "heavy rock music", like Led Zeppelin, so they said. They were Daniele Davoli, Mirko Limoni and Valerio Semplici. They had samplers, synths, emulators and imagination to take any song snippet, turn it around, bend it to their will and make the perfect high energy dance record. That is what they did, but they had a little unaccredited help along the way.

In 1980 American singer Loleatta Holloway put out a single called "Love Sensation" produced by Dan Hartman. The first version of "Ride on Time" sampled her vocals and some of the music track from "Love Sensation" without any permission obtained. Daniele Davoli had thought Ms Holloway was dead and there would be no issues, only to then find out she was very much alive, by which time it was too late and "Ride", with her vocals on, was already out. Loleatta and Dan not surprisingly sued and obtained a rather large out of court settlement. Black Box did apologise, something they had to do quite a lot during this period. This version was retained for a 1990 album called Dreamland, where Loleatta and Dan are both credited and therefore received royalties. I reckon they both did doubly well financially in the end. That was quite right too.

So, a version with a new singer was then recorded for the '89 single. This featured new and upcoming vocalist, Heather Small, soon to be famous as the singer with M People. She did her version in just one hour and was not told why she was suddenly being used as a replacement vocalist for Loleatta. I think her vocals are stunning and it is this aural version that was heard (if not seen!) on TOTP during its six-week run at No. 1 in autumn '89.

Just when you thought it was safe to go back outside, the deception got worse. Heather did not appear on TOTP singing her part. Black Box hired in Katrin Quinol to lip-sync Heather, who had redone Loleatta. That makes Katrin two times removed as the original vocalist. Her job was to dance around, look good and sell the record, which she did with great energy and synchronicity with the vocal track. Unfortunately, Black Box were to have similar vocalist problems soon after "Ride on Time". They were very keen on the odd bit of lip-syncing and not crediting singers!

"Ride on Time" was still a very great single though. I have to keep saying this to remind myself, despite the issues. If you forget these, close your eyes, then just dance and scream, undulating all over the dance floor, without falling over, then you can just appreciate what a wonderful memorable single it was. If the record buying public had known about these issues at the time, would they still have bought it? I think the answer is yes. It had great musical hooks with some of Loleatta/Heather/not Katrin vocals, nice disco rhythms with pulsating grandiose synthesised chords. It just makes you "wanna" dance and sing, wave your arms in the air again and again. It was a great feel-good record for a grey rainy day, as autumn and winter took over in late '89, with its infectious high energy. It is a song that is memorable and not forgettable, like all good pop songs. It's cliché time. It is not surprising it got to No. 1.

Lyrically there is nothing too strenuously complex. It is all self-explanatory saying you are a "hot sensation" on the dance floor and it's party time. The rumour was that the track should have been called "Right on Time", but our Italian producers got their English mixed up. "Ride on Time" is just so much cooler and enigmatic. It was a good mistake to make.

During the making of the 1989 Dreamland album, Black Box employed singer Martha Wash to produce demo versions of six songs for the album. This she did quite happily, only to find out later that she was singing on the final tracks and was not credited and therefore not paid appropriately. For publicity and promotional purposes Katrin Quinol was back leaping around and lip-syncing again. Martha was able to settle out of court for a large sum in 1990. Since these halcyon days of hits and lawsuits, Black Box have carried on with music with a new vocalist, Charvoni Woodson, from the '90s, who sang on the records and performed live with Black Box until 2018. They have never achieved the level of success that they obtained in the lip-syncing early years.

With Black Box being so successful in '89-90, it makes you wonder just why they did not just credit people properly and get a proper singer in. It is not that they needed to save money. However, they did shell a lot of it out in financial settlements. In my mind it was all a very strange affair and therefore one of the more unusual and bizarre No. 1s in this book. It was still a great single though!

Chapter 27

Vogue: Madonna

Released 20 March 1990
No. 1 for 3 weeks
14 April to 28 April '90
Sales UK: 663,000

Love her or loathe her, you just cannot ignore Madonna, a woman and recording artist who collects superlatives for fun. She has sold 300m musical units worldwide, has had 13 No. 1s in the UK and is the most successful female singer, in terms of sales, of all time. Her music and influence have touched on social, political religious and sexual themes. Throughout her career she has produced great pop, often with an experimental twist. She has transcended beyond music and become a dominant and controversial figure in popular culture in a now forty plus year career of being a world-famous icon. In the '80s, to some extent my lost decade in music, I was still aware of Madonna and was quite easily impressed, especially as I thought she was quite sexy. In the circles I mixed with it was not done to say you found her hot or even lukewarm, either musically or visually. On this theme of sex, it became very clear Madonna was in control of her own sexuality as promotion for the music. This had not happened in the past, where pop and film stars had flaunted themselves in this way to attract publicity, at the behest of men. She came over in all aspects of her life as very much the one in charge of her own actions. In the '80s, America had Madonna, we had Margaret Thatcher — a strange comparison? Probably, but both women were absolute control freaks, neither was an easy collaborator, both were quite domineering over male colleagues, and they transcended their chosen profession to something beyond pop music and politics. Maybe we should just be grateful Mrs Thatcher did not make pop records, although Madonna might have made a fun Prime Minister in giving tax breaks to nightclubs.

Pre-1990, when "Vogue" came out, Madonna already had No. 1s with "Into the Groove" in '85 and "Papa Don't Preach" and "True Blue" in '86. This was then followed by "La Isla Bonita" and "Who's That Girl" in '87 and finally the religiously controversial "Like a Prayer" in '89. Madonna, like Kevin Rowland from Dexys in '82 (see Chapter 19) and Neil Tennant of the Pet Shop Boys (see Chapter 24) in '87, had a Catholic upbringing and the influence of that religion came through in the lyrics of "Like a Prayer". However, my early Madonna favourite was "Holiday" for its great Latin groove from '84, which I still play for fun to this day.

"Vogue" came out in March 1990 and subsequently got to No. 1 during the next month for three weeks. It topped the charts in many parts of the world, eventually selling 6m copies across the globe. It came from the soundtrack album "I'm Breathless" which had the music from the Dick Tracy film Madonna had just starred in. Having said that, "Vogue" itself was not featured in the film but it became the leadoff single from the album.

In the '80s in gay clubs in New York there was a type of dance called Vogue or Voguing, where the participants moved around but occasionally would stop dead still and "strike a pose". Lyrically then, this was Madonna's subject matter, basically saying "life can be grim but never mind let's go dancing" and then when on the dance floor "let your body go with the flow" and then "strike a pose". I particularly like the rap bit mentioning Greta Garbo and Marilyn Monroe, among others, which comes in at 3:40 minutes during the 4:53 minutes long single. All in all, there were over 70 lines of lyrics, mainly repetitive, but they scan well in the song.

Musically the track is very typical of the '80s. Madonna was assisted here by producer Shep Pettibone in the writing and arrangement. Multiple keyboards were used with synthesised strings, piano and drum machines but like many other '80s entries on our list there was no electric guitar, as it was felt the ubiquitous keyboard could do everything. It would take Britpop in the UK and Grunge in America to bring the electric guitar back into the pop mainstream. Minus this instrument, "Vogue" still had this amazing groove and danceability. It is another single that is very memorable, unforgettable and still played everywhere to this day.

One of the lines in the song says, "it makes no difference if you are black or white" (a Michael Jackson lyric also) and this line was taken by Madonna to create and produce a 20 hour video made for the single filmed in… black and white! Very effective it was too. Having not seen the video for years till researching this chapter, I actually remembered it, as not having colour was a great gimmick that made the video stand out as being different.

There is absolutely no doubt this is a great song, a worthy and obvious No. 1 from one of the greatest artists of all time. Madonna has carried on with hits to the present day, never disappearing, remaining controversial and having some health issues in recent years. Of her later stuff, I really liked "Hung Up" from 2005, where she sampled "Gimme! Gimme! Gimme!" from ABBA. Madonna is still part of the global collective consciousness in the 2020s and she is not finished yet. Meanwhile, I am finished for this chapter. I am off to have a cup of tea and then "strike a pose" before the next one.

Chapter 28

(Everything I Do), I Do It for You: Bryan Adams

Released 17 June 1991
No. 1 for 16 weeks
13 July to 26 October '91
Sales UK: 1.87m

There is a well-known Canadian photographer, who just happens to also be a famous philanthropist, charity fundraiser, animal rights campaigner and prominent vegan. In his spare time, he has written the odd and also very good zillion selling pop single, among other musical adventures. Welcome to the whole life of Bryan Adams, rock and pop star and electric guitar player (formerly an endangered species, having not seen many guitars in the '80s No. 1s). Yet he still only got the second longest ever weekly No. 1 run in the UK singles charts, a bit lightweight you might think? Not really Bryan, I am only joking.

Bryan started to make a name for himself in the '80s, mainly in North America with some hard-hitting rock records such as the 1983 album Cuts like a Knife, and in '84 the album Reckless. This spawned two famous hits "Run to You", which I was rather partial to and "Summer of '69". His image was very much the "chap next door in tee-shirt and jeans, who picks up an electric guitar, makes a record, so what, it's no big deal". They were good pop rock songs and there was not (much) of an '80s synth in sight. However, by 1991 Bryans was about to have the very, very big one!

"(Everything I Do), I Do It for You" was written by Bryan, Michael Kamen and Robert John "Mutt" Lange in 45 minutes in March 1991. It was included on two albums, the first was on the soundtrack for the Robin Hood: Prince of Thieves film and the second was on Bryan's own album, Waking Up the Neighbours. Performing on it were Bryan on vocals and guitar, Bill Payne on

Piano, Keith Scott on lead guitar and backing vocals, Mickey Curry on drums, Larry Klein on bass, Robbie King on organ and finally Mutt Lange on some synths. After years of hits with synths, emulators, machines, computers and technocrats, real instruments were back!

This is where the superb superlatives start. It is true it was only the second longest No. 1 but it was consecutive without a break, being at the top for 16 weeks in one go, from July to October '91. Frankie Laine in 1953 got to No. 1 with "I Believe" for nine weeks, then there was a one-week break. It went back to the top for another six weeks and finally after another one-week break, it went to No. 1 for another three weeks; 18 in all but not consecutively like "I Do". This was No. 1 in 19 countries, selling 15m copies worldwide. It was voted the 18th best song of all time in the UK in a Guinness Book of Records poll. It also won a Grammy for the best motion picture song for 1991. All this for a soppy little ballad, that everyone loved; even I did, on a good day.

The musical track is piano led at the start with clear, precise, heartfelt singing by Bryan. Drums and guitar thunder in at 1 minute and the lyrics are interrupted eventually towards the end by a stately, concise, melodic guitar solo. This is more or less the first No. 1 to have a solo of this type, since Bohemian Rhapsody in '75, the '80s being a guitar-free zone. The energy of the instrumentation, especially the booming bass drum every 4th beat emphasises the song's power ballad credentials.

Lyrically it is a simple love song, with lovingly devotional lyrics, there is nothing ironic, and nothing enigmatic with words that everybody could understand and relate to.

It is undeniably a great song of its type, being the ultimate power ballad. Should it really have deserved to be No. 1 for so long though? Well maybe yes! It was tied in with a very successful film, had a great melody and was wonderfully well produced with heartfelt sincere lyrics of universal appeal. It also depends on what else was around in the charts at the time and it was a bit of a slow summer for other hits. I thought it was good, but funnily enough I did prefer "Love Is All Around" from Wet Wet Wet (see Chapter 31), out a few years later, which had a similar chart experience and was also a love song. There is no denying "I Do's" credibility and lasting appeal though to this day. A super worthy No. 1!

Bryan Adams continued to put out the hits in terms of albums and singles, but he has become so much more over the years and become another transcendental pop star like Madonna! He is a photographer of some repute and has even done album covers, for example for Annie Lennox's The Annie Lennox Collection. Some years ago, he set up The Bryan Adams Foundation Charity, which he mainly self-funds. This has helped causes all over the world. One UK example is paying for a new playground at the Park Walk Primary School in London in 2019. He has also been an animal rights campaigner for some years, and he is well known for being a vegan.

Bryan is obviously a top chap in all aspects of his life. Personally, he comes over as an everyman who has the common touch — meant as a compliment — to be relatable to just about anyone, as an entertainer and human being. "(Everything I Do), I Do It for You" was just so unpretentious, simple and straight down the line; again, that is meant as a compliment. It did exactly what it said on the tin but did it so much better than everybody else. If we ever have a World President, then I would vote for Bryan Adams.

Chapter 29

Deeply Dippy: Right Said Fred

Released 9 March 1992
No. 1 for 3 weeks
18 April to 2 May '82
Sales UK: 200,000

Actor Bernard Cribbins, as a young man, put out a single in 1962 called "Right Said Fred". I can find no evidence that Right Said Fred in return put a single out called "Bernard Cribbins". If so, and it got to No. 1, the course of history could have been changed. A song about a much-loved British national treasure might have been No. 1 for at least four weeks, compared to the three weeks of "Deeply Dippy". I don't suppose Bernard minded too much, but maybe he should have got some royalties from Right Said Fred's record sales. As it happened, we had to settle for "Deeply Dippy", which was a song about "curves, fun and passion", very much the typical pop song sentiment. I don't mean to be too rude about this song. It was jaunty, cheerful, bouncy and saxy, with a great solo from said instrument. Compared with some No. 1s on my list, which shall be nameless but are coming up very soon, "Dippy" is one of the best songs of all time!

Right Said Fred were formed in 1989 by the Fairbrass brothers, Richard on vocals and bass, with younger brother Fred playing guitar. They had both been in a '70s rock band called the Actors. The brothers were soon augmented by second guitarist Rob Manzoli and adopted the Right Said Fred moniker.

By 1991, Richard and Fred also owned a gym in London and were consistently amazed by young sexy 20-something people working out there, with supermodel looks and bodies. They all loved posing in their tight Lycra at the gym apparently, even on occasions removing their tops, when everybody was looking. So, they wrote a soon to be famous song "I'm Too Sexy" about these narcissistic tendencies among their clientele. This, of course, is nonsense. Richard and Fred were muscle-bound hunks and were only too keen on TOTP and elsewhere to open and remove their shirts at every opportunity to flaunt their bulging pecs and biceps. It was a song about them. "Sexy" was a great simple fun record, through a catchy melody, with Richard's rich baritone bass voice dominating the track. It was very much a No. 1, but Bryan Adams from the last chapter had other ideas. "Sexy" stalled at No. 2 behind "(Everything I Do), I Do It for You" for weeks and that was that in the UK. However, it did top the Billboard singles charts in America.

"Don't Talk Just Kiss" was their second single, being more in the same vein and did well, getting to No. 3 in October '81. When "Dippy" came out in March '92, it was No. 1 for three weeks in April/May. "I Do" from Bryan was not at the top anymore by then so of course everyone else was in with a chance. "Dippy" was also No. 1 in Ireland for four weeks but did not do much else in other countries.

It was a cool song, acoustic guitar driven, highlighting again the power of Richard's voice but the best bit for me anyway was always going to be the mid song sax solo by Molly Duncan with full band joining in enthusiastically. "Dippy" was very much a sing-along song, with foot tapping and to make a change from air guitar, you could play air sax. It was very much an audience participation song. The whole track has a sleazy, jazzy, good mood feel. In other words, it was not half bad!

Lyrically not much was happening, the words could be a little sexy or a little decadent or a little nothing. That perhaps did not matter though as it was a song with such a smooth groove. For me it passed me by at the time, but I can see why it was a hit at No. 1 and I really like the saxy bit on listening again all these years later. Also, by this time in '82, Right Said Fred had a big momentum from their previous singles to encourage big sales for "Dippy".

The video was a fun, glorious, very colourful affair with multiple costume changes and settings. It was a huge change in style from the black and white video for "Vogue" for Madonna in 1990 but it worked well to promote the music for "Dippy".

Right Said Fred had an album called Up put out in '92, which had all three singles on and sold well. They had a final top 10 hit with the "in your face" title of "Stick It Out" in '94. The rather risqué title was in a good cause for Comic Relief. Those few golden years in the early '90s were it for Right Said Fred at the very top. However, Richard and Fred have carried on their merry way since, here, there and everywhere with their music. However, some rather controversial views on Covid vaccines, the Russia-Ukraine War and climate change might have dampened their sales and appeal somewhat in recent years.

It is a strange contrast between Bryan Adams from the last chapter and the Fairbrass brothers; one is approaching sainthood, while Richard and Fred have in the eyes of some, just gone a bit "dippy" themselves. But in '91-92 they were far too sexy for the charts and their music gave pleasure to millions. That is how they will hopefully be remembered.

Chapter 30

Mr Blobby: Mr Blobby

Released 9 November 1993
No. 1 for 1 week 11 December '93,
then for 2 weeks 25 December '93 to 1 January '94
Sales UK: 600,000

As indicated in the Intro, I have had some correspondence from Mr Blobby regarding this single. He has indicated to me that I have to be careful as to what I say about his famous song, that he will accept the title of "best worst No. 1 song of all time", just not "the worst worst song of all time" in any critique I might make. Any further denigration of said song will result in a severe squishing for me, so he has said. Mr B had also insisted on proofreading this chapter in the company of his lawyer, so a little care is needed with my comments.

It is an absolute and true fact and not a conspiracy theory that Mr Blobby was No. 1 for three weeks over the Christmas period of 1993. It is also nearly an absolute fact that no one, including Mr B himself, knows quite why. Time to try and find out.

Mr Blobby was invented by Charlie Adams, a production assistant for BBC's Noel's House Party. He was played in costume by Shakespearian actor Barry Killerby in the early years. Barry was to remark just how uncomfortable and exhausting the Blobby costume was, however, the diktat is that you always have to suffer for your art. It could have been worse playing a Dalek or Cyberman on Dr Who, which would not have been much fun. His Blobbiness was championed, promoted and eulogised by Noel Edmonds on Noel's House Party, as a new figure to entertain the nation. For those of you too traumatised to remember, The Blob was a bulbous pink figure, with yellow spots, a toothy grin and green jiggling eyes. He had an extensive vocabulary, where he could say "blobby" in different frequencies, tones, dialects and languages. He was very much an all-round polymath and intellectual giant. Blob Person's career took off from the House Party, from where he went to take up cameo roles on Lovejoy and Keeping Up Appearances, amongst other BBC programmes. Sir Blobby also appeared as a candidate in the Littleborough and Saddleworth by-election, Lancashire in 1995, getting 105 votes (that was 0.2% of the total) and failing miserably to be elected. However, he did, of course, sell considerably more than 105 singles in 1993.

Mr Blobby certainly appealed to children whether aged 3 or perhaps 33. He just seemed to be everywhere across the media and the airways. He was very much an irritating sensation, or was perhaps just sensationally irritating. On one public appearance he destroyed a young girl's cake as an act of blobbishness, presumably meant to be funny, only to be then physically attacked by the angry girl's father as an act of attempted blobbicide. He was either very funny with very English ridiculous humour and was "a right laugh" or conversely totally stupid, grotesquely annoying and should have been removed from our screens to preserve the nation's sanity immediately. However, whatever your views, it was always time for another comedy single.

Having just watched the song video again after 30 years, I am pleased to say I made it to the end with sanity intact, just! I grudgingly admit the video is very funny in places and features a plethora of well-known Blobite acolytes such as Jeremy Clarkson. It also involved song parodies such as "Addicted to Love" by Robert Palmer where the heavyweight pink Superblob collapses on to the drums and destroys the set, ho, ho?

As for the music, it was written by Philip Raxster and produced by Paul Shaw and David Rogers. Legend has it that in 1994 they were paid further monies to not do "Mr Blobby 2", as the follow-up single. It actually displaced "I'd Do Anything for Love (But I Won't Do That)" sung by Meat Loaf and written by

Jim Steinman. This was one of those "pocket" symphony No. 1s that everybody loved. The music track for "Mr Blobby" featured a sort of whimsical childish fairground organ sound with children singing and vocalists warbling with profound lyrics from The Blob dissecting and elucidating on the human condition. Or that would have been the case, if the Blobbyfied sounds could have been translated.

The critics, to be blunt, were utterly scathing in their comments on the single. "Worst of all time" is one of the nicer ones. Yet in our crazy mixed up story of chart No. 1s, "Mr Blobby" was a topper like "Combine" ('76) and "The Chicken Song" ('86). As before, everybody seems to love a comedy record. In this case I would guess it was parents, who were buying the single in droves, as a stocking filler for their children. If it was not Christmas, I suspect it would not have got to No. 1.

It was a poor riposte to some of the previous year's great Xmas top hits. It is certainly not memorable in the way that many No. 1s in this book are. The worst No. 1 of all time is probably, in the eyes of many, correct. Sorry Lord Blobby, I cannot even call it "the best worst of all time". However, at the time of Xmas 1993 it did give fun and seasonal joy to under-3s everywhere. For that it must be seriously and comically praised! Meanwhile, I am expecting a backlash or squishlash from the Blobster for my comments, as he will probably not agree, and I cannot let him proofread and destroy the chapter. So, I am now going into hiding for several months before attempting the next chapter. If you see Mr Blobby, simply tell him I have left the building.

Chapter 31

Love Is All Around: Wet Wet Wet

Released 9 May 1994
No. 1 for 15 weeks
4 June to 10 September '94
Sales UK: 1.91m

In 1970 a disintegrating rock group, big in the '60s, had a studio row about the recording of a new track, ironically called "Tranquillity". The tape was running, and the conversation was recorded, to reveal a 12-minute "swearathon" where the singer denigrated the drummer in particular in a very unpleasant rant about his percussive playing. Eventually, to great notoriety, the Troggs Tapes of the row were released, merely to enhance the reputation of the Troggs as a "wild things" band and as proto punks. Eventually singer Reg Presley and drummer Ronnie Bond kissed, made up and agreed their argument was very entertaining, in showing that bands do row in the privacy of the studio, suggesting the ranting can be cathartic for future band relationships. It was fortuitous that the argument just happened to be recorded. A few years earlier the Troggs had released "Wild Thing", a sexy, sleazy, rocky, brute of a track and a famous hit in 1967. If you took the Troggs Tapes and "Wild Thing" in isolation, you would see that Reg was a rocker, shouter and all-round hard man. You did not want to mess with him. But nice little "two sides" Reg had a sensitive, lovey-dovey, nurturing side, being a true romantic. In 1967 he just went and casually wrote one of the greatest love songs of all time, but he had to wait till 1994 to find out just how great it was. The Troggs' hit with "Love Is All Around" had got to a respectable No. 5 in November '67 but it was the cover by Wet Wet Wet that took it to another level into the stratosphere 27 years later.

Wet Wet Wet had been formed in Glasgow in the early '80s by the main man Mark McLachlan, soon to be known as Marti Pellow. They were going to be called Wet Wet only but decided a triple Wet sounded cooler and a bit different. Their breakthrough album was Holding Back the River in 1989 with the hit single "Sweet Surrender" which got to No. 6. The Wets already had a No. 1 with a Beatle cover "With a Little Help from My Friends", a joint double A side charity single for Childline, with Billy Bragg, as the other artist who covered the Beatles' "She's Leaving Home" in 1988. In '92 "Goodnight Girl" was a No. 1 single taken from the album High on the Happy Side. "Love Is All Around" or "I Will Survive" by Gloria Gaynor, amongst other songs, was offered to Wet Wet Wet by producer Richard Curtis of Four Weddings and a Funeral as part of the soundtrack album for that film. Fortunately for this chapter, The Wets chose "Love" over "Survive", which may not have had the same staying at the top power.

Reg Presley had written the song in about 10 minutes, so he claims, and The Wets took the song, making it their own with a different intro and outro. It was released in May '94 and was immediately loved by the public and critics alike. It got to the top and stayed there for nearly ever, 15 weeks, one less then Bryan Adams's "I Do" from '91, but then it sold more singles (1.91m to 1.87m). There was talk across the land that towards the end of the song's reign at the top, that radio stations were not playing it anymore because people were getting tired of it. However, that may be not really true as "Love" was still selling in its zillions and was still very popular. Finally, The Wets themselves withdrew it from commercial circulation in week 15. Playing on the single were Marti Pellow on vocals, Graeme Duffin on guitar, Neil Mitchell on keyboards, Tommy Cunningham on drums and Graeme Clark on bass, with the eternally happily grateful Reg Presley on exceedingly huge extra songwriting royalties. These he has used to fund his extracurricular research career into crop circles and paranormal activity since '94.

Musically I would describe the Troggs' '67 version as steady, having no real peaks or troughs, and it flows along nicely, getting the job done. Reg Presley's vocals are sort of melancholy, as if he can't quite believe his luck that he might just get the girl in the end. However, The Wets version takes off, especially at the start and end in a way the Troggy one does not. Marti Pellow's vocals are clear but very emotional and full of yearning and pleading for the girl to bend to his romantic vision. Both the intro and outro use lead guitar, which is very well played and enhances the track. The guitar is definitely now back for the '90s and will be even more so next year and in the next chapter. The '80s "just synth" days seem well and truly gone.

Lyrically here the heartfelt words are important. They are simple and very relatable and apply to anyone who has ever been in love, which is practically all of us. It is always a very popular karaoke track, perhaps not though, if you have been spurned.

I did and still do really like "Love" more so than Bryan Adams's "I Do", which is the obvious song to make a comparison to. Perhaps as musical chart punters, we were just so lucky to have two great universal love songs out within three years of each other.

Wet Wet Wet carried on, as all these bands do, who have had the biggie and then do not quite reach the same heights again. They had three further top 5 singles in the late '90s and then faded away gradually. "Love Is All Around" is a great memorable song and a worthy No. 1. It will be played on the Earth, Moon, Mars and all points celestial, for a long time into our human future. However, my advice is to avoid at all costs, if you ever come across it, my karaoke version.

Chapter 32

Some Might Say: Oasis

Released 24 April 1995
No. 1 for 1 week
6 May '95
Sales UK: 458,000

An oasis is an unusually wet area within a desert, such as the Sahara, which is surrounded by palm trees. Often a small settlement will arise in these areas, attracted by an abundant source of water, where there is none generally to be found in the wider area. Oasis is also a ladies clothing firm specialising in colourful feminine fashionable attire. Oasis is again well known as a soft drink, concentrating on tropical colourful fruits, with a tangy, tickly, fizzy taste to brighten your day. The ultimate Oasis was, however, a leisure centre in Swindon, England that sadly closed permanently during the Covid pandemic in 2020.

So, the quiz question is: just which one of these types of Oasis did Liam Gallagher name his new band after in 1991? Oasis obsessives will know that the bedroom that Liam and Noel shared as children had a Manchester band, Inspiral Carpets poster on the wall, which mentioned a tour gig list, There was no mention of a desert, soft drinks or fashionable clothes either as a venue or giving tour sponsorship on the poster. One of the gigs was to take place at said Oasis Leisure Centre in Swindon. Thus, the fable goes, as to how the band were named after a leisure centre, very rock'n'roll (not)!

In 1991 Liam on vocals got together with Paul "Bonehead" Arthurs on guitar, Paul McGuigan on bass, and Tony McCarroll on drums. Noel G had actually been working as a roadie for the aforementioned Inspiral Carpets and joined the band a little later. Immediately, due to extreme talent, he took over Oasis's songwriting and became the de facto bandleader. By '94 they had hit the big time in the album charts with Definitely Maybe, which got to No. 1. They were also very media friendly, as Noel in particular was always good value, entertainingly outspoken and controversial in interviews. They also had a bit of a hedonistic lifestyle, liking a drink, a toke and a snort and on a good night even a fight, which got them more publicity, as the then bad boys of rock'n'roll. It did not stop the great music, which I really liked at the time. Just like the Beatles and the Stones in the '60s there was also a supposed rivalry with "soft" southerners Blur for pole positions in the chart. In reality, both bands got on well. Blur's first No. 1 "Country House" got to the top in August '95, which was slightly behind that of Oasis' first No. 1, being "Some Might Say" in May '95.

"Some Might Say" was written in March '95 and put out in April. It was also featured on Oasis' second album (What's The Story) Morning Glory? that also got to No. 1 in the album charts. "Some" was very much of its time. The music track was grungy, rocky, very amplified and dominated by Liam's "in your face, don't mess with me" voice. There was no keyboard, a one hundred percent turnaround from the synth dominated '80s. Maybe the last time in our No. 1 list that there was no keyboard was back in the '60s with the Beatles "I Want to Hold Your Hand" in '64 and the Stones with "Satisfaction" in '65. Noel claimed his original demo version for the band to learn was even dirtier and sleazy sounding than the actual released single. I liked "Some", it was bouncy and headbangable, along with some entertainingly nonsense lyrics. It was years later that I heard the B side of "Some" for the first time, which was "Acquiesce" which in my view is just brilliant, one of the best Oasis songs ever. They appeared twice on TOTP with "Some", once with Tony McCarroll on drums, while on the second occasion with new boy Alan White banging the sticks. The Gallaghers did not rate Tony any more as a drummer, but at least he got performing royalties from playing "Some" in the studio.

Lyrically I am not sure what to think. Are they deep meaningful lyrics that say something profound about the human condition? I just can't fathom them out, or are they nonsense? They are also fun though. Try "sink is full of fishes, She has got dirty dishes on the brain" which always makes me laugh as a ridiculously funny line. Maybe the lyrics don't matter. Some writers like being enigmatic and mysterious and when you pin them down about their own lyrics, they haven't got a clue either. Try listening to some '70s prog rock bands, if you like being confused. In fairness to Noel, his lyrics did become more accessible and relatable in time. Consider the heartfelt, wonderful positive lyrics to "Don't Look Back In Anger" for example.

Oasis eventually had eight No. 1 singles, and "Some" was up there with best of them, but maybe their greatest song of all, "Wonderwall", only got to No. 2. I mentioned this in the Intro to the book, that along with "Penny Lane/Strawberry Fields" by the Beatles, this could be up there with the best songs of all time to not get to No. 1. There could be another book in this, something like "Wonder Penny: 27 No. 2 Great Songs That Should Have Got to the Top".

Unlike many other bands in our list, Oasis became "many hit wonders" and carried on to 2009, when Noel and Liam had their final bust-up of many. Noel left and subsequently the whole band split. Rather sadly, the two warring brothers still don't really talk to each other but "some might say" it would be great if they did and got back together all these years later and "did not look back in anger". I would pay good money to see them together live. At least they both perform solo and still sing some of these wonderful songs on stage. Long live rock'n'roll and long live Liam'n'Noel!

Chapter 33

Wannabe: Spice Girls

Released 26 June 1996
No. 1 for 7 weeks
27 July to 7 September '96
Sales UK: 1.38m

The early to mid '90s saw the rise of Britpop. Here, guitar bands made a comeback playing essentially rock music that was able to penetrate the pop chart mainstream. This was dominated and exemplified by Oasis and Blur. It was all possibly associated with lads who bought Loaded and FHM magazine, who liked a drink or seven on a Friday night. Meanwhile and simultaneously was the rise of the boy bands. Take That, Boyzone and Westlife dominated, where the chaps did not play instruments or generally write their own songs. Gary Barlow as a piano player and writer for Take That was a talented outlier and exception. In a way, the boy bands were like '60s soul vocal harmony groups such as the Four Tops and the Temptations, who with slick production and presentation, appealed just as much to girls and boys, who preferred a softer poppy approach. However, where were the bands populated by girls, who wrote for girls (and men in touch with their feminine side), to vocalise on feminine issues and concerns? By 1995 the pop world was therefore ripe for takeover by the rise of the females. It took, at first, a management company called Heart which put the Spice Girls together, after auditions and then a new manager supreme Simon Fuller to make it happen. When it did, girl power was to take over big time!

The Spice Girls are so ingrained in the national psyche and the author's psyche that I do not even have to look up their names and monikers. After all these years I still know them. They were Melanie Brown as Scary Spice, Melanie Chisholm as

Sporty Spice, Emma Bunton as Baby Spice, Victoria Adams (now Beckham) as Posh Spice and Geri Halliwell as Ginger Spice. Their band personas were lively, wacky, sexy, confident and very much in control. Like Madonna earlier, they seemed to be calling the shots, not the men behind them. For girls from 12 to perhaps 40 they were a wonderful breath of fresh air. By 1996 they had a No. 1 album, Spice, which had four No. 1 singles off it, including the "wanna wanna zigazig ah" song, "Wannabe", the first to rise to the top.

"Wannabe" was written by the Spices, along with Matt Rowe and Richard "Biff" Stannard. The legend has it that it was written in 30 minutes, as all the best songs are, and then recorded in one hour. It was put out in June '96 and was No. 1 for seven weeks over the summer school holidays. "Wannabe" got the Brit award for best single of '96 and it got to No. 1 on the USA billboard charts for three weeks in January '97. Not bad for a track where the girls appear desperate to avoid sneezing (see next but one paragraph)!

Musically the track is lively, with a simple accessible, bouncy melody. It is piano-led and with synths and strings and no guitar, but then it did not need it. Mel B and Geri lead with raps but all the others have their moments, perhaps apart from Victoria who was not present in the studio during the main recording. Her backing vocals were added later. It was not rock as we know it, but the single encompasses rap, hip-hop, dance and pop to great effect.

The lyrics are very simple to explain, I hope. They imply that lovers come and go but friendships last forever. If you did want to be my lover, then my girly gang will have to vet you. We, the Spice Girls are such a tight unit, that you may struggle to fit in. My favourite line though is "I wanna really wanna zigazig ah!" which always suggests to me as the line approaches its climax, that the poor girls are just desperate to…er… sneeze big time! I am sure my accurate and intellectual analysis of that lyric is absolutely spot on, or perhaps maybe not?

The video was shot in the Midland Grand Hotel just outside St Pancras Station in London. It has one continuous shot and shows the girls running around, singing, dancing and getting up to mischief but in a wholesome fun way, never being nasty. It all looks very spontaneous, but allegedly was rehearsed for hours before being filmed.

By 1996 I was over 40 years old and pop music was beginning to pass me by, but you could not avoid the Spices. They were "in your face" and just everywhere, being newsworthy as well as pop worthy. "Wannabe" was ok for me; I appreciated its pop sensibilities and can understand very easily why it got to No. 1 and then stayed there for quite a while. After playing it again all these years later, the tune is lodged in my brain. I can't forget it, which always indicates a single's staying power. Luckily, it has dislodged Mr Blobby, our '93 entry in the book, at last from my music-retaining grey matter, so that is good. Sorry Blobster!

After "Wannabe" the Spice Girls continued to dominate through the '90s, with seven further No. 1s, so they were never going to recede into the distance quietly. They paved the way for other girl bands who followed, including Girls Aloud, All Saints and the Sugar Babes, along with the explosion and dominance more generally of female "girl power" artists in the charts. The Spices are now the biggest selling UK act since the Beatles and across the world are the biggest selling girl band of all time with 105m record sales. All because they toyed around and invented a new little phrase we all now know and love. With that I will "zigazig ah" you, till the next chapter.

Chapter 34

Candle in the Wind '97: Elton John

Released 13 September 1997
No. 1 for 5 weeks
20 September to 18 October '97
Sales UK: 5m

Our story for this song starts way back in 1926, when Norma Jeane Mortenson was born. She grew up to be a voluptuous beautiful young woman, eventually becoming a film star and changing her name to Marilyn Monroe. In her roles, she played the blonde bombshell sex symbol to perfection, in movies like The Seven Year Itch from 1955 and Some Like It Hot from 1959. She was not short of male attention and had two starstruck marriages, the first being to baseball payer Joe DiMaggio, the second was to playwright Arthur Miller. Both ended in divorce. However, Marilyn's life was not trouble free. Unlike, say Madonna years later, who was able to manipulate her own sexuality to promote herself, Marilyn's sexuality was exploited for commercial purposes solely by men. She became very stressed with mental health issues and turned to drink and drugs for some relief. She eventually died of a supposed barbiturate overdose in 1962, aged just 36. It may have been a suicide. Conspiracy theories abound here. Marilyn Monroe at that time was universally loved across America and it was a great shock across the nation when she died. Just perhaps she was the nearest to a "princess" the USA ever got to, in terms of adoration, love and respect. Does it remind you of someone similar perhaps, closer to home?

Bernie Taupin, lyricist for Elton John, was fascinated by the rich and famous, who often had troubled lives. If these people were a flame, it would be constantly flickering and liable to be blown out very easily. They were living such fragile lives.

Their lives were like a "candle in the wind". He chose Marilyn as his subject and thus "Candle in the Wind" the 1973 version was born. Elton John sang and recorded it with his then band, Davey Johnstone on guitar, Dee Murray on bass and Nigel Olsson on drums. The band complements Elton's singing and piano playing, especially Davey's often underrated guitar playing, whose lead lines respond to Elton's sympathetic singing perfectly. The lyrics are a warm heartfelt tribute to Marilyn, full of empathy and understanding. The match between music and lyrics is just perfect; the best there ever was according to Bernie, when he and Elton did songs together. It came from the parent album Goodbye Yellow Brick Road, a big seller, which explains probably why "Candle" only got to No. 11 in the UK singles chart in '73. A very popular Elton song over the years, he has played this version live 1,706 times between 1973 and 2023.

There have quite rightly so, been millions of words of tribute written about Diana, Princess of Wales, but here is a short summary. As Lady Diana Spencer she married Prince Charles in 1981 in a lavish ceremony in Westminster Abbey. She had two children with Charles: William and Harry, and very soon developed her own independent profile, as a working, very popular member of the royal family. She very much had the common touch with ordinary people, in being able to relate to their lives in a warm and empathetic way, that perhaps other members of the royal family could not. Therefore, when her marriage to Charles broke up, it was her that got sympathy, not him. By '97 she was in a newish relationship with Dodi Fayed and out and about in Paris on the last day of August of that year. There is no doubt that Diana was hounded and pursued ruthlessly by the press for tittle tattle and gossip and that evening was no exception. A car she was being driven in crashed in an underpass in Paris, killing her and Dodi more or less instantly. The car had been speeding to escape the pursuit of the following press pack. She was 36 when she died, exactly the same age as Marilyn Monroe.

The funeral was set for the 6th of September at Westminster Abbey. Richard Branson asked Elton and Bernie to redo "Candle in the Wind" as a tribute to Diana, by changing the lyrics. They had very little time to do this, as Elton was to sing the new version at the funeral. This he did with great dignity, his voice sounding appropriately delicate, yet strong. This was the only time he was ever to play this version live. He and Diana had been friends and fallen out, then made up by the time of her death, so Elton very much meant every word! The mass crowd listening through speakers outside were very moved by the song and it was now obvious it would be released as a single with all proceeds going to Diana's favoured charities. It came out a week after the funeral, backed as a double A side with "Something About the Way You Look Tonight" a song, through no fault of its own, no one really remembers. It was only No. 1 in the UK for five weeks, yet sold just about 5m copies making it the UK's biggest ever single. It was also No. 1 for 14 weeks in the USA and eventually sold across the world a fantastic 33m copies, putting it second of all time to "White Christmas" by Bing Crosby, which over nearly 80 years has sold 50m.

The music track for "Candle in the Wind '97" is sparser than the 1973 version, with piano, which Elton embellishes accompanied by a backing string synth track. Elton's voice is again sensitively strong, and George Martin of Beatle Fame produced the whole song.

"Goodbye England's rose" is the opening line and like those of the earlier version for Marilyn, the lyrics are heartfelt, warm and empathetic, as they should be. If I had to make any comment here then Diana was the Princess of Wales and the royal family represents Great Britain, yet the lyrics only reference England. Maybe "Britain" or "British" did not scan well in the song. However, this is a just a minor quibble and the song and its sentiment did everybody proud!

I remember the time as a massive national outpouring of grief for Diana. Was it over the top? Probably not, as it was a cathartic moment for the nation and a moment of great togetherness, with the funeral being a unifying, universally accepted event. Diana was generally loved by all and had become a true "national treasure"! It did take the royal family some time to recover from this, as they were not considered to have treated Diana well. There are some similarities between Marilyn and Diana. Both were very attractive, both were vulnerable with mental health problems, and both were mistreated by those around them, yet were loved by their nations' populations. "Candle in the Wind" was the perfect song for both women. However, the song and its sentiment live on forever in this country, as a fitting tribute to Diana. Her legacy lives on not least in her two children, William and Harry. "Candle in the Wind '97" is just about the most blatantly obvious and deserving No. 1 that has ever been written.

Chapter 35

Millennium: Robbie Williams

Released 7 September 1998
No. 1 for 1 week
19 September '98
Sales UK: 400,000

The Bond Bug Car was a two-seater, three-wheeled car built by the Reliant Motor Company in the 1970s, similar but smaller to the three-wheeled backfiring van used by Del and Rodney in the famous BBC sitcom Only Fools and Horses. The Aston Martin DB5 is an iconic historical British motorcar produced in the 1960s. This was the one driven by super spy, British secret service agent, James Bond. The other was driven by a once obscure wannabe pop star, who came from Stoke-on-Trent and for his misdemeanours supported Walsall Football Club. His name was Robert Peter Williams and by the time of the video, he was doing quite well.

The above paragraph is a reference to the video for Robbie's single "Millennium" and vividly illustrates his capacity for "self-deprecating" humour. He also very much had the common touch in being able to relate to people, which are perhaps his two greatest traits. He could have an awkward side though. We would all perhaps like Robbie as a neighbour. It could be fun. However, Jimmy Page of Led Zeppelin fame, Robbie's next-door neighbour has objected to the plan to expand the Robster's house in London, in adding on an underground swimming pool and gym, an issue that seems to have dragged on for years. I am sure it could all be settled over a nice hot cup of green tea, now come on chaps!

Robbie was already famous as a member of the first big boy band Take That for five years between 1990 and '95. He rather lost his way for a while, being photographed drunk and debilitated, out carousing hedonistically with bands like Oasis. After a lost year in '96, he was able to hit the big time in '97. His breakthrough was with the album, Life thru a Lens, which had a No. 4 hit on it called "Angels". I suspect you may have heard of this one, but did you know that by 2005 a poll had placed it among the nation's favourite funeral songs? "Let Me Entertain You", more of a trumpet solo rocker, also got to No. 3 from the same album. "Angels" was never a No. 1, surprisingly, yet it is still his most famous song. It was the '98 album, I've Been Expecting You that produced "Millennium" as his first No. 1 hit single.

The song was initially written by Robbie and long-term musical partner Guy Chambers, who played just about every instrument on the music track, apart from drums which were played by Chris Sharrok. The song also incorporates the musical hook from the 1967 Bond Hit "You Only Live Twice" sung then by Nancy Sinatra and written by John Barry for music and Leslie Bricusse for the then lyrics. Both these two chaps get writing credits. The London Session Orchestra added classical overdubs on later. Like supposedly many No. 1s, it was written in a short time period and just thrown together in four hours. For those musos amongst you it only comprises two chords and is in the key of D flat major, which is unusual for a pop song. Compared to some of the more recent and very famous '90s No. 1s, it was not a massive seller, but it still got to the top for one week in September '98.

Listening to the music track it is quite simple; it is steady, even paced and linear without any great musical peaks and to my undiscerning ears almost a bit boring. I find it is impossible to listen to the single without thinking of the wonderful video that goes with it. My view is that the music is smooth, moody and vaguely memorable, while the video is so very memorable! It was probably that which got the single to No. 1. This is surely one of the best examples of a great video, propelling and selling a slightly weaker single to the top of the charts, recollected in this book.

Lyrically it is another weird one, hinting at ideas such as "take a pause in your life, slow down, find yourself a partner and think for yourself" I think? I don't claim ever to be an expert on all lyrics. I think I became dazed and confused in early adulthood listening to the convoluted lyrics in prog rock bands of the '70s and have never recovered fully. Anyway, Robbie and Guy are being enigmatic here and the mood music of "Millennium" is enhanced by the words, which at the end of the day, was possibly what the two writers wanted.

The video is of course a James Bond-like affair. Robbie plays roulette, gets the girls while doing his best Sean Connery, James Bond impersonation in his white tuxedo. Look more closely and you can see the join in the studio speedboat scene, with the added on later seascape. The whole video is a deliberate parody and all the more funny for it. But the real highlight and punchline is when Robbie drives off in the Bond Bug three-wheeler at the end, only to break down and be overtaken by the Aston Martin DB5.

Robbie went on to huge fame and fortune, becoming a multi-hit wonder. He has had seven No. 1 singles, 13 No. 1 albums, 18 Brit awards, and 77m albums being sold worldwide. He could do no wrong in the charts, despite some personal issues in his private life. In 2010 he rejoined Take That for a while, to great further acclaim. On a side or skin note Robbie is a big fan of tattoos. A strange one was of the very heavy metal band Motörhead, who were about as far away from his musical tastes as Mr Blobby was from being able to sing. Apologies King Blob! Robbie is yet another great pop star to have a hint of a "national treasure" about him. He does come over a regular "everyman" guy. Everyone still loves him to this day, well perhaps apart from Jimmy Page.

Chapter 36

Livin' la Vida Loca: Ricky Martin

Released 27 March 1999
No. 1 for 3weeks
17 July to 31 July '99
Sales UK: 352,000

Enrique Ricky Martin Morales, otherwise known as Ricky Martin, could be described as (more or less) a one hit wonder in the UK but this would be a little unfair. Across the world in both Spanish and English singing markets, he has sold up to 70m records, from the early '90s. I just wonder if there is anybody, anywhere, at any time, who would not dance or sing to "Livin' la Vida Loca", when hearing it. It is such a good, energetic, universally accepted, feel-good record. It could even encourage me to dance and exclaim "wow" on a bad day, it is that toe-tapping. In 1999 I was still generally obsessed with classic rock, so liking "Loca" must be our little secret. Mind you, under any definition of the word, Ricky rocks! Also, this song is a dance and pop music extravaganza of electrifying energy and "Loca" is almost irritatingly irresistible! While you let my over-the-top hyperboles die down, here is a bit more about Ricky.

He was born in 1971 in Puerto Rica, growing up in a Spanish speaking household and having musical heroes such as Madonna for pop, Gloria Estefan for Latin and Carlos Santana for rock. By the early '90s he was a Spanish language ballad singer but to go big, like others before, he had to break out into English language singing. This is what he did with the 1999 album Ricky Martin that included "Loca".

"Livin' la Vida Loca" means, "living the crazy life". Draco Rosa and Desmond Child wrote it. It got to the top of the Billboard American charts for five weeks, while going big here for three weeks in July. A Latin version also topped the Billboard

Latin charts in the USA. Like "Millennium" in the last chapter, the fantastically supercharged energetic video only promoted the song to greater sales. The critic fell in love with "Loca". "Electrifying", "full of life", "sexy", "super danceable" were some of their more understated comments.

The music track was very slick; my favourite bit was the low non-screechy lead guitar lines, in response to Ricky's inflamed passionate vocals. Rhythmically it was just such a fantastic groove, up there with "Billy Jean" from '83 by Michael Jackson in our other No. 1s in the book, for sheer dancing power.

Lyrically it was all-just "livewire, go for it, have lots of hedonistic fun, if you were tough enough". The woman at the centre of Ricky's attention was obviously the most sensual, beautiful, lively, sexy woman history had ever known and you would have a great time with her, providing you could keep up, without taking any stimulating drugs.

The video was just brilliant to watch. Some of the synchronised fast Latin salsa dancing had to be seen to be believed. Ricky is very much in charge, dominating the action as the male sex symbol and loving every minute. All very exciting but a personal gripe here is that no camera shot lasts for more than about three seconds, this being true of many later pop videos. It can all be a bit overpowering for someone of my delicate disposition and advanced age. I am also totally exhausted just watching the video for "Loca" again, all these years later.

I do like this song and will admit more or less willingly, to dancing and singing along, when no one is looking. It is very obvious just why it got to No. 1, but just in case I shall reiterate. Fun, danceable, feel-good factor, entertaining lyrics, great video, drop-dead gorgeous man (my wife tells me he is super sexy?), all very well presented where "Loca" is definitely not just a victory for style over substance. That should about cover it.

Ricky carried on with the hits across the world. In 2000 he had a No. 4 hit with "She Bangs" — a song in similar style and sentiment to "Loca", without quite the same energy and impact. It is worth noting that Ricky, despite his heterosexual cavorting in the "Loca" video, eventually came out as gay and is a great supporter of LGBT causes round the world. In 2004 he also set up a charity, The Ricky Martin Foundation, which acts to fight against human trafficking. He is definitely an all-round good bloke as well as great singer. Most people in the UK will only remember him for one song, "Livin' la Vida Loca", but when your biggie is as wonderful as that, there can be no complaints. Keep on "living the crazy life" Ricky!

Chapter 37

Spinning Around: Kylie Minogue

Released 19 June 20
No. 1 for 1 week
1 July 2000
Sales UK: 400,000

If you just happened to be in Melbourne, Australia and decided to pop into the Performing Arts Collection Museum at the Arts Centre there, you could observe, with great interest, a pair of gold hot pants once worn by the next super iconic person to fill our No. 1 list. It was not the Spice Girls, Madonna or even Mick Jagger. It was in fact the world record holder for the "sexiest female bum of all time", if you believed the papers and the hype. Even I noticed this, in my oncoming and withering older age when I saw the music video to Spinning Around in 2000. Sex sells records and it was a chap called William Baker, the superstar's stylist, who decided to put the "world's best bum" in gold hot pants, which were allegedly bought for 50p. I don't believe that one, I bet they were a bit pricey and made to measure. The hot pants, subsequently washed, ironed and brushed up to perfection, were displayed in various exhibitions over the years, celebrating the famous wearer before fetching up in Melbourne. Enough of this nonsense! The wearer just happened to be a marvellous singer, athletic dancer, consummate pop star and very nice person, no matter what she wore. She has continued to be so over the last 40 years. Welcome the wonderful Kylie Minogue to your chapter in our book!

Kylie's back-story is well known. As a late teenager, Australian soap Neighbours was her break. From that she was adopted by the Stock, Aitken and Waterman production and writing team in the UK, who in 1988 wrote Kylie's first No. 1 single "I Should Be So Lucky". Soon after this, she did a great version of Little Eva's "The Loco-Motion", first out in 1962, which got to No. 2. For the next few years Kylie was all over the UK charts with further No. 1s such as "Tears on My Pillow" in 1990. By the later '90s, she began to move away from dance pop to become more experimental and interesting, but selling considerably fewer records. Eventually, her then record label Destruction records dropped her. She got a new deal with Parlophone (the Beatles original label) and decided wisely to go back to what she did best, dance pop.

"Spinning Around" was originally meant for Paula Abdul, who had cowritten the song. That did not materialise, and it ended up with Kylie. Paula, Ira Shickman, Osbourne Bingham and Kara DioGuardi wrote the song together. It was put out in June and virtually a week later it was No. 1, selling 82,000 copies, while at the top for just one week. This became Kylie's fifth No. 1. "Spinning's" eventual sales were about 400,000. It was very much a pop dance disco track, having the same style and sentiment as Ricky "Latin" Martin's "Loca" topper from the last chapter. It was made to be a feel-good, bouncy, fun, sexy and pure escapist single for a great time at the start of the new millennium.

Musically the track is piano and keyboard dominated without a guitar in earshot. It is impeccably well produced but very much a typical dance pop track. The lyrics are more interesting though. "Have a good time, yes, but it is always the time to make a clean start and learn from your mistake" is what they seem to be saying, while having a great dance out of course.

The video, which stars that iconically famous clothing attire and co-stars Kylie is otherwise a standard night club "we are all having a good time" film. At that time, performance elaborate dance orientated videos were all the rage and no doubt this approach took "Spinning" to greater commercial heights as well as getting all the participants very fit. Kylie's live performances of the song, over the years, are exuberant, great feel-good participation events, where pop star, dancers, band

and audience have a great shared experience. Kylie is a bit more sensibly dressed (but not much) in singing "Spinning" at these live gigs, to preserve her modesty.

It was another obvious No. 1 with a memorable, unforgettable tune and is still performed today. It is a bit too poppy for me and contrived, where maybe style has slightly triumphed over substance but if you like Kylie and fun pop music, then this is not half bad, and you will love it.

After "Spinning Around" Kylie became part of the pop, cultural and social landscape. Like Madonna before her, she transcended being a mere pop star. By 2001 she had the top hit "Can't Get You Out of My Head", a No. 1 for four weeks over September and October, which sold about 500,000 copies in just a month. In 2005 she took a year out to successfully battle breast cancer with help from a great outpouring of public support. Since then, it has been Kylie business as usual, with music, TV (Vicar of Dibley, Dr Who) and many films (Jack and Diane: 2012 and Galavant: 2015 are two examples). Her costumes and very camp performing sensibilities have made her again, like Madonna before, a favourite with the gay community. Basically, everybody loves her; she still has the girl next-door image appearing to be accessible and a good friend to relate to but at the same time coming over as sexy and sophisticated. As an Australian, she has to be a "guest" national treasure in the UK or perhaps she could be visiting prime minister for a few months? I would vote for her, especially if she dug out those gold hot pants on the campaign trail. Right, probably a good moment to stop this chapter right there!

Chapter 38

Mambo No. 5: Bob the Builder

Released 3 September 2001
No. 1 for 1 week
15 September 2001
Sales UK: 400,000

By 2001 it could be argued not much had changed with the charts since 1964. TOTP was still watched by millions, the singles market was still healthy, and the great songs would still get to the topmost of the time. Amazingly, over the years the children's novelty comedy song still was able to go all the way on occasions, even at this later stage in chart history. It is almost like the normal record buying public stay at home and a totally new set of punters come out to play, in this case parents, buying for their children. Just how many people who bought "Spinning Around" last year from Kylie for pleasure would buy "Mambo No. 5" by Bob the Builder for pleasure? Probably absolutely none, but they would have bought it for their own children or someone else's children. Like other similar records, it originated with a TV series. In listening now to dear old Neil Morrissey singing Bob for this chapter, I cannot ever recall hearing "Mambo No. 5" in 2001 but then again, I was 46 years young at the time but still not quite young enough for Bob. It is quite cute and likable and a little different from other recent No. 1s in the book. It also got to the top without it being Christmas.

Keith Chapman created Bob the Builder for Hit Entertainment and Hot Animation. It tells the story of Bob and his friend and colleague Wendy, who do good wholesome building deeds to make the world a better place. It reminds me of the TV show, DIY SOS fronted by Nick Knowles, who will renovate and change people's houses in a worthy feel-good way to change people's lives for the better. Nick did not have various dumper trucks and vehicles though to help, which Bob did, nor was he animated, as Bob was. These building machines were called Scoop, Dizzy, Roley, Muck and Lofty being very cute characters and only too happy to help. Worthy qualities like conflict resolution, cooperation and socialisation were all highlighted in the show. I must now apologise for even suggesting if I gave Bob a negative review of "Mambo No. 5", he would brick me up behind a wall, which I mentioned in the Intro: A Book Start. Bob is not that sort of boy, being far more morally sound and promoting more wholesome good deeds than I realised. Not for him the destructive anarchist tendencies originating from that silly spotty Blob from 1993. By late 2000 Bob was the biggest thing on CBBC and just ripe for a record release. This happened with "Can We Fix It" being released in December, topping the charts over Xmas 2000 and still being No. 1 in early January. "Mambo No. 5" was to come out in September 2001.

"Mambo No. 5" was written as a jazzy dance instrumental by Cuban, Dámaso Pérez Prado in 1949 This original is only just over two minutes, having some whooping vocalisations and energetic use of brass instruments and is fun. The next version was "A Little Bit of Mambo" from Lou Bega, an Italian Ugandan living in Germany in 1999. This used snippets and motifs from the original but claimed itself to be a (more or less) new song. Lou claimed sole copyright for writing, but the estate of Dámaso Pérez Prado counterclaimed, then won and were given joint songwriting credits for "Mambo". This version is entertaining in a mamboish sort of way, being a big hit across Europe, getting to No. 1 here in September '99. I may be a little sad, but I actually prefer Bob's version to Lou's.

Neil Morrissey sings it in a very good deadpan non-cool rap voice, with backing vocals from Rob Rackstraw and Kate Harbour. It is really effective as a novelty hit for children and dumper drivers everywhere. The light, poppy backing is very suitable and appropriate for the child-friendly mood that is required. But the highlight for me is the start, where the vocalists do a parody of "Ballroom Blitz" by Sweet, which to my extreme embarrassment made me laugh out loud! Lyrically it is all straightforward lyrics about well, building things. There is nothing enigmatic, ironic or sexual in the words, you get what it says on the tin or dumper.

The halcyon days of Bob are long gone but I feel this was a sweet moment and relevant footnote in chart history for Bob to savour. It is a lightweight song, yet it is not arrogant in tone, it is not "in your face" and not so silly that it makes Mr Blobby seem like Shakespeare or Bob Dylan. Mambo No. 5 has an air of childlike innocence about it, which makes it a very endearing and quite charming song.

Chapter 39

A Little Less Conversation: Elvis vs JXL

Released 10 June 2002
No. 1 for 4 weeks
29 June to 13 July 2002
Sales UK: 800,000

Elvis never really left the building in 1977. In fact, there is an elderly, white haired gentleman, living just down the road from me, who swears he is Elvis and works down the local chip shop on a Wednesday and Thursday. He works as an Elvis impersonator in care homes for geriatrics at the weekends. Elvis Presley, the legend, will of course never die and he was immortalised in the chip shop song in 1981 by Kirsty MacColl in "There's a Guy Works Down the Chip Shop Swears He's Elvis". His cultural and social impact as a giant musical icon of the 20th century will live on forever. He was able, effortlessly, to move across the genres of pop, country rockabilly, and R'n'B selling over 300m records in the process, including the most No. 1s by any artist in the UK. You can take your pick from your favourite Elvis song, maybe for me, it would be "Suspicious Minds", which amazingly only got to No. 2 in 1969.

JXL was the pseudonym of a Dutch DJ, composer, multi-instrumentalist, producer and all-round musical polymath called Tom Holkenborg. By 2002 he was in his early 20s and had been influenced growing up by a mix of musical styles including prog rock, dance and electronica. He was later to work with Hans Zimmer on film scores such as for The Dark Knight Rises and Man of Steel. He was very much a different character from Elvis but looking at his CV, he is still a very busy man today. Yet the two men were to collaborate on a massive No. 1 hit, not that Elvis knew too much about it by 2002.

This is the first No. 1 I have featured that has been reworked as a remix. This is where the original song is taken and rearranged in a different way. The vocals might be brought up into the mix or the drums enhanced, or extra percussion is added. Often extra drum machine tracks are added to boost up the rhythm section to make it more danceable to play in clubs. This is what happened with "A Little". The remix is not a cover; the basic song is still there and recognisable. Sometimes a remix can be quite subtle, you may not see the join, but in our case the difference was noticeable.

The original "A Little Less Conversation" was written in 1968 by Mac Davis and Billy Strange and recorded by Elvis in March that year for a comeback TV special. It is lively, energetic, having a great dance groove and very much appropriate for Elvis the Pelvis's hip thrusts and cool moves. As per usual, Elvis's rich, baritone, sexy (so I am told) voice dominates the song. It was not released as a single in the UK and was therefore not a hit back in '68.

In 2001, the original song had been used in a film called Ocean's Eleven and was becoming well known again by the public. Therefore in 2002, Junkie XL, as Tom Holkenborg was then known, took the song with the permission of the Presley estate and added more guitar, more horns and uprated the drums and percussion. In other words, he gave it a cloudscape that was common for the 21st century. You can clearly hear the join, yet the music track is far funkier with added groove. It even makes me "wanna" get up and just dance. It was around this time it was suggested to Tom that he should get rid of the "Junkie" part of his name as it was pointed this could be associated with the sad circumstances of Elvis's death. This he did, becoming just a 'J' as in JXL. The XL bit, so Tom said, stood for expanding limits, which is certainly what he did for Elvis with the remix. This version was released in June, becoming No. 1 in thirteen countries, including in the UK for four weeks.

Well as for the lyrics, really? They are very sexist and retro! Basically, Elvis is saying "don't talk, don't procrastinate, grab your coat, back to mine, let's get it on". They are very '60s lyrics, where the man is the sexual predator, and the woman is submissive. You perhaps would not find them in a song now. Mind you of course this was Elvis the Pelvis we were talking about, perhaps "the sexiest man of all time", so he could just about get away with it.

As for the remix song, does it add to the original? It is certainly funkier and rocks more, but I am not sure I can tell too much difference. It was a lively, bouncy, dancey, funky pop song, which would be played in discos and clubs as a dance track, possibly with the lyrics becoming irrelevant. The video is very slick, modern for 2002 and filled with young people dancing energetically. Again, the video was perhaps better than the song and certainly helped sell more copies. "A Little" had eventually morphed into a modern dance record and that probably gives it the unique selling point to explain it getting to the top. If you forget about the slightly dodgy sexist lyrics, then it could be a great idea to spend three minutes and 40 seconds of the rest of your life listening to the song, while working out and dancing.

Gustav Mahler

Chapter 40

Crazy in Love: Beyoncé

Released 14 May 2003
No. 1 for 3 weeks
12 July to 26 July 2003
Sales UK: 2.4m

It has been noticeable journeying through this book that in the past, songs had one writer or possibly two at the most. With Elton John for example, he would do the music, while Bernie Taupin would write the lyrics. By the noughties, this had changed, songwriting teams came about, often as a result of sampling. This would involve maybe only taking a few seconds of an old song, as a musical hook or motif to then be incorporated into the new song. The writer(s) of the historical song would need to be credited as well. John Bonham, of Led Zeppelin, has had his drum sound sampled hundreds of times, including a considerable number from just one song "When the Levee Breaks". On one occasion this involved Beyoncé on her song from 2016 called "Don't Hurt Yourself". Because of this, the four members of Led Zeppelin are credited as writers plus Jack White, Diana Gordon and Beyoncé herself, which on my last count makes seven people to make a four-minute rock pop song. There are of course, issues with copyright if past writers aren't credited, but it does make you wonder if there is anything original left to write when you have to use old music. The ultimate point is, I suppose, that the songs still sound great and the singles will sell like hot cakes.

"Crazy in Love" had four writers and it worked like this. Rich Harrison (producer, writer and multi-instrumentalist) came up with the bare bones of a song but could not find the hook, the musical punch line, until he remembered a track from 1970 by the Chi-Lites called "Are You My Woman? (Tell Me So)" written then by Eugene Record. He duly sampled the motif he needed and thus Eugene, 23 years after the original, got a writing credit in 2003. Rich then took the track for Beyoncé to sing and record and she added the bridge. In a song, this makes up the short bit in the middle that links the two halves of the song together, so she gets a writing credit. It was felt by Rich and Beyoncé it just needed a little more, that killer touch to send it over the edge as a big seller. In pops Beyoncé's husband, rapper Jay-Z, to record a brief rap recorded in about half an hour, to complete the song. The main writer here is very much Rich Harrison, but it is interesting to see how the song was put together. "Crazy in Love" did quite well in the end, even if a committee appeared to write it.

The song has been described as having pop, hip-hop, R'n'B, soul and funk all in one package. It is certainly lively, energetically sexy with super percussive and horn playing effects, while not being super-fast, only cruising at 100 bpm. You could strut to it, as well as dance. The video is just very typical of the early noughties. There is lots of action, lots of vibrant colour and some crazy jerkily dramatic "pulled muscle" dancing. Beyoncé changes costume umpteen times including into a leotard that luckily for us; Jay-Z does not wear while standing still, delivering the rap. After a car explodes, health and safety take note, a fire hydrant breaks, making Beyoncé very wet and see-through. It is not, of course, that sex was being used to help sell the record!

Lyrically the song is all about a man who is driving Beyoncé "crazy in love", how she misses him, when he is not there. It is very much relatable lyrics again, every pop song's favourite topic being boy/girl relationships and why not, it is something most of us can relate to at some time in our lives.

"Crazy in Love" is impeccably well produced, very slickly presented and the combination of song and video is perfect. The mood, feel and style of the song are overpowering and maybe are another case where the lyrics don't matter too much? Is it all just too perfect and maybe too easy? Music and video technology was such that by 2003 you could more or less create what you wanted without a blemish in sight. The same criteria apply in live performances, all totally spotless and shiny. I think "ultra professional" are the words I am looking for.

In our chart story, "Crazy in Love" is still a great song, being danceable, relatable and therefore sellable in huge quantities. The eventual final sales for "Crazy in Love" were huge, over 2 m in the UK.

Beyoncé has sold over 200m records and has 32 Grammy awards. Her own heroes were Michael Jackson, Tina Turner, Diana Ross, Madonna, and also because she was a black woman of substance, Michelle Obama. She has also supported the Black Lives Matter campaign and been involved in numerous philanthropic good works with charities. Basically, she is an all-round good egg with a huge following and immense popularity.

Classical composer Gustav Mahler born in eastern Bohemia, then part of the Austrian Empire, would have approved. It is one of those million-dollar quiz questions: which famous classical composer was a very distant relative of Beyoncé? The answer is Mahler as he and Beyoncé were cousins four times removed. He lived in Germany and died in 1911, so they never met. If they had, in between writing symphonies, Gustav would no doubt be orchestrating and producing our singer's next single and would be adding himself to the writing team.

Chapter 41

Call on Me: Eric Prydz

Released 13 September 2004
No. 1 for 3 weeks 18 September to 2 October,
then for 2 weeks 23 October to 30 October 2004
Sales UK: 300,000

This book is not about the videos that went with many of our singles. However, whereas in the early days they were there to be produced as "back up" to the aural singles, by the early noughties they were definitely there to "front up" the songs. In 1975 "Bohemian Rhapsody" came out with its then groundbreaking video. This was to enable the song to be played in the TOTP studio, when Queen were not able to be there live. This was the famous singing heads video with a "live" performance film at the beginning and end of the song. The video could be considered as a "supplementary addition" to "Bo Rhap", not having yet equal status with the song itself. By the '80s with the advent of MTV in the USA, videos could be played elsewhere other than just pop shows and be more widely seen, as promotional tools. This decade could perhaps be when video creativity was at its zenith, with mini films that could be even considered works of substantive art. My favourite video of this type would be in 1986 for "Sledgehammer" by Peter Gabriel, created by Aardman Animations with its Wallace and Gromit-like living plasticine.

By the noughties there were so many pop video channels available to many people on satellite TV, that at this stage, video had (finally) killed the radio star. People often got the first hearing and sight of a new song through the video channels, rather than through the radio. Therefore, the video had to be good to be able to front load commercially for the single. For "Call on Me" the video became (in)famous for either being "the

5th worst video of all time", as described by the New Musical Express, or "the sexiest video of all time" as described by almost everybody else.

It was perhaps also the first song on our list where the supposed main writer had very little to do with actually creating the music and where the main body of work for the track was a super sample! Whereas taking a few seconds for a hook or motif could be pinched here, as with "Crazy in Love" by Beyoncé (see Chapter 40), "Call on Me" was a wholesale mega snatch of another song.

In 1982 Steve Winwood wrote the music and Will Jennings penned the lyrics for a single called "Valerie" from a Winwood album called Talking Back to the Night. Lyrically it was a tale of the singer seeking to find a lost love. This was "Valerie", probably based on real life singer Valerie Carter. It was though just a minor hit, getting to No. 51 in the singles chart. There was nothing minor about Steve Winwood, he was a giant in the rock world. He was the main man, as keyboard player, great soulful singer and writer in first the Spencer Davis Group and then secondly in Traffic. As a solo performer he has continued to release critically acclaimed albums to this day. Yet a major contribution to pop culture, along with his rock god status, has to be that he wrote the main musical parts for a No. 1 dance song played in clubs and fitness classes everywhere.

"Valerie" had been taken by Thomas Bangalter from Daft Punk and producer, DJ Falcon and then sampled for a live dance DJ mix in clubs. However, they did not put it out as a single but passed it on to Swedish DJ Eric Prydz, who did. This gave writing credits to Steve Winwood, Will Jennings and Eric Prydz. He rhymed "Call on Me" with "Valerie", tweaked the melody, drum machined the rhythm and made a typical noughties dance track. Steve was so impressed with Eric's effort that he re-recorded his "Valerie" vocals to become "Call on Me". Therefore, a member of the rock aristocracy had sung on a single about to become famous as the song in "the sexiest video ever".

This is a truly bizarre event. Have you no shame, serious artist Steve Winwood?

In 1983 Duran Duran had a hit with "Girls on Film" and this was promoted by a very sexualised video that got banned. Naturally, I have not seen this video... well not for about 30 years, but it was banned during daylight hours and its notoriety sold the single. Therefore, the typical music video began to take a sex angle about as far as it could without getting banned, as sex was able to sell big time. Even if said video was banned, it might still be a good unique selling point. This concept was taken to the ultimate limit by "Call on Me".

Back in the '80s, the aerobic fitness craze was all Jane Fonda leggings, headbands and thong leotards. Women loved doing it and men loved to watch, so I have been told, and our featured video took this as its starting idea. It was a fitness class work out to "Call on Me", where the women were all wearing variations of '80s Lycra. The main female dancer was Australian choreographer Deanne Berry who spent the whole time pouting. There was one man, Juan Pablo Di Pace, who joined in the class and spent the whole time smirking. I cannot think why? As this book is written before the watershed, I will only describe the dance moves of having a thrusting nature, involving the sort of gymnastic elastic body movement that is likely to cause serious injury. So don't try this at home or if you do, don't film it and put it out on video... on the other hand? I will stop there. I am sure you get the idea!

Having watched the video just recently, just the once only for research purposes, it is sexy, and entertaining. The girl's facial expressions and pouts are very funny. It is also "blatantly in your face", maybe over the top and should not be watched by the under 60s or alternatively perhaps the over 60s. The actual music track sounds good, well produced and the "Valerie/Call on Me" hook is the big sing-along moment. It got to No. 1 for five weeks in total, in a block of three weeks, then two weeks, interrupted by Robbie Williams, with his single "Radio".

Deanne and the dancing girls put out a fitness video on the back of "Call on Me" called predictably "Pump It Up", which I absolutely, categorically deny ever seeing. Eric continued on his merry way with his music career, doing a sampled version of Pink Floyd's "Another Brick in the Wall" (see Chapter 44) called "Proper Education" amongst other sampling.

One final thought for this chapter is just how grateful we should all be, that no one made an "up front" video for "Je T'aime... Moi Non Plus" in 1969 (Chapter 6). Can you just imagine? It is probably best not to!

Chapter 42

(Is This the Way to) Amarillo: Tony Christie with Peter Kay

Released 14 March 2005
No. 1 for 7 weeks
26 March to 7 May 2005
Sales UK: 1.2m

This was a re-release of an old song, with no remixing or sampling or sexy video, being very much a throwback to the (good/bad) old days of pure pop. Peter Kay is not on the single at all in an aural sense but featured big time on the video as director of operations and as walk leader. It was a charity single for Comic Relief in 2005 and it rightly sold a lot of copies. It was noncontroversial and a great sing-along. It raised lots of money, was great fun and even I could dumb down and specialise in the "sha la la la la la la la" karaoke lyrics, with a hand clap at the end. Yes, there were seven "la las", I counted them in and I counted them out. There was one little unforeseen hiccup with "Amarillo", which I will come to later.

Tony Christie (born Anthony Fitzgerald in 1943) was just about the archetypal, easy listening, middle of the road pop star coming through in the 1960s and '70s. His big hit was "I Did What I Did for Maria" in '71, which got to No. 2. "Amarillo" also put out that year, surprisingly only got to No. 18. Tony continued to work, always perhaps on the fringes of the big-time success, through to the early 2000s and then afterwards.

"(Is This the Way to) Amarillo" was written by Neil Sedaka and Howard Greenfield in the '60s. Neil only put his own version out in 1977, which was a minor hit in the USA, only getting to No. 44 on the Billboard charts. Neil and Howard wanted a country and western feel to the song and were influenced by "Hitchin' a Ride" by Vanity Fare. The original destination was going to be Pensacola rather than Amarillo, still with four syllables but perhaps not quite so catchy. They were able to give the song to Tony in 1971. Lyrically the poor singer cannot find his way to Amarillo where his girl Marie is waiting. This was of course before the days of sat nav, and there was never a policeman around to ask for directions, when you wanted one. This is another song with quite sad lyrics, yet a bouncy, jaunty, foot-tapping melody.

Meanwhile, Peter Kay was born in 1973, two years after "Amarillo" first came out. He is an actor, writer, director and very funny comedian. I tend to think of him as the "eh by gum, it's grim up north" equivalent of soft southerner James Corden in the original way he tackles comedy. In 2002 he had come to prominence in Phoenix Nights, the Channel 4 sitcom and everybody liked him. I certainly did. In his stand-up routine, he does misheard song lyrics, which having seen him doing this online always makes me laugh out loud.

The video for "Amarillo" was very much about Peter. He mimes to the song walking along, joined by a plethora of famous faces including William Roache and Anne Kirkbride from Coronation Street (Ken and Deirdre), Ronnie Corbett, Michael Parkinson, Jim Bowen, and Shaun and Bez from the Happy Mondays. With big apologies to anyone I have missed out. Oh, all right then, as it was for charity, I have to mention the pink and yellow spotted terror and very special guest in "Amarillo", Mr Blobby. It is funny, entertaining and very much the case of just how many stars can you spot in 3.33 minutes? Even Tony Christie himself puts in only a small cameo appearance on his own song, but it was in a good cause, so I don't suppose he minded.

On a more serious note, Jimmy Savile had a walk on part as well in 2005 but post-2012 was edited out of the video, quite rightly so, when his crimes became apparent. Unfortunately, he still had a role to play on the last ever TOTP a year later, as I mentioned in the Intro to the book.

Peter went on to two more charity singles with "I'm Gonna Be (500 miles)" by the Proclaimers, which he actually sang on, in 2007 and also "The Official BBC Children in Need Medley" in 2009. This also brought back a contribution from everybody's favourite builder Bob, from Chapter 38, ably voiced again by Neil Morrissey.

The three charity singles in my list from Band Aid, Elton, and Tony have all been massive sellers, not surprisingly. "Amarillo" was the biggest selling single of 2005. It is therefore obvious just why they were all No. 1s. "Amarillo" has no remixing, no sampling and no sexy video, but was a classic pop single that would have been bought by everybody of all ages, in a good cause. The single was very retro and old fashioned in its feel. But just when you think I am turning into an old fuddy duddy "better in my day" type, our final year 2006 entry was back to pop, dance, sex and glamour and it was not half bad! Read on folks.

Chapter 43

Hips Don't Lie: Shakira with Wyclef Jean

Released 14 February 2006
No. 1 for 1 week 8 July 2006,
then for 4 weeks 5 August to 26 August 2006
Sales UK: 1m

By 2006 I was not watching TOTP or taking much interest in the singles chart. Therefore, I was not aware of "Hips Don't Lie" at the time. However, listening to it now for this book, I have been pleasantly surprised as to just how good it is and how much I like it. I work out with weights at home and either play prog rock from my favourite band Jethro Tull, or I will play zumba, salsa dance tracks which quite frankly are more likely to get me lifting bigger weights than the no dance, arty, serious "stiff upper lip" music of Tull. I absolutely love the polyrhythms and percussive nature of the zumba stuff, finding it so energising. The musical Latin pop term is a reggaeton beat and of course this is present in a big way with "Hips" as well. In combination with great singing and presentation, I think this song is probably my favourite of all the pop dance tracks on my list of No. 1s. Luckily for me and the rest of the world, I do not try and impersonate Shakira's hips dance movement, while lifting weights. If I did, I would not be able to walk again, never mind work out.

The single was unusual in that it got to No. 1, then took three weeks off and then went back to No. 1 for four weeks. When the last TOTP went out on the 30th of July, "Hips" was considered to be No. 1 on the show, even though technically it did not officially get back to the top until the 5th of August, hence it being written about in this chapter. Otherwise, I could have done "Don't Stop Me Now" by McFly, a great cover of the Queen song but not as interesting as the "Hips" story.

Shakira Isabel Mebarak Ripoll was born in 1977 and was a Columbian of Lebanese descent. She has been able to incorporate both East and West musical motifs into her music and has sold over 100m records, which puts her up there with other female mega sellers on our No. 1 list, like Madonna, Kylie and Beyoncé. She was, is, and will continue to be a superstar of pop.

"Hips Don't Lie" came from Shakira's seventh album, Oral Fixation, Vol. 2 and as was typical of the time, it had a complex writing history. The original idea came from percussion player Archie Pena, who worked up the basic music and lyrics with Shakira. Wyclef Jean, the Haitian rapper, had an earlier song called "Dance Like This" which was reworked for "Hips", so he and his original cowriter, Omar Alfanno on "Dance" also get writing credits. I do hope you are keeping up. Jerry Duplessis, who helped out on production as well, also gets a writing credit as does a LaTavia Parker and a Luis Dias. I think that makes seven writers in all, but it is quite tricky to work out who did what and when. It was very much the trend by the noughties, for songs to be written by committee and for your poor scribe it all gets a bit confusing. I give my apologies to any obscure Latin, dance, producer, DJ, remixer person who also may have made a contribution that I might have missed out. Anyway, I like it and it was a mega hit getting to the top in 17 countries. Up to the present day it has sold 13m copies globally of both real and downloaded origin.

The music track just maybe has some "chukka chukka" rhythmic guitar in the background but otherwise it is all synths, programmes and multiple percussion tracks. It is an infectious mix and despite the fact I am, as I write, a 68-year-old intellectual, untrendy, "hips do lie" male, I just "wanna dance dance dance" when I hear "Hips" Do I need help or at least perhaps a hip replacement?

The lyrics are a conversation between a woman and a man and how they are both driving each other crazy with lust; pretty standard fare for pop dance songs of the noughties. My favourite line is along the lines of "when she dances like this, she makes a man want to speak Spanish". Ultimately, as indicated in other songs, with such a vibrant, overpowering, dominating dance track do the lyrics matter though? The video is also very much of its time, colourful, vibrant and dancey and is a fun watch. This was another great song that made it naturally and deservedly to the top.

I am pleased I have arrived at my 43rd song 43 years after "I Want to Hold Your Hand" in 1964. I like both tracks, perhaps "Hand" from the Fab Four, a bit more. It is perhaps fitting over the years, whatever the fashion, trend and culture, that you can't keep a good song down. I wonder though, just how wonderful a combined mash up or interweaved sampling of "Hand" and "Hips" would be to make one "new" song? Now there would be a challenge! It would have Lennon and McCartney as cowriters plus the five from "Hips" making seven in all and probably be No. 1 forever.

Bonus Tracks

Chapter 44

1979: Another Brick in the Wall: Pink Floyd

Released 23 November 1979
No. 1 for 5 weeks
15 December '79 to 12 January '80
Sales UK: 1m

Pink Floyd did not do singles. Roger Waters, chief songwriter, made this quite clear to producer Bob Ezrin, when he suggested taking a song fragment called "Another Brick in the Wall, Part 2", then doubling it in length, putting on a disco beat and even more bizarrely putting on a children's choir to sing the repeated lyrics. Roger and Dave Gilmour, the other main man in Floyd agreed, not at that time even thinking about a single, never mind a No. 1 massive seller. Pink Floyd were a serious "thinking about the human condition", art, prog rock band specially created for nerds like me, and they did not do singles!

Well they did, in the past, but it was a long time ago. In 1967 Dave had not yet joined the band and guitar and song writing was courtesy of the legend that was Syd Barrett, who had pop sensibilities and was happy to write '60s psychedelic hits. These were "Arnold Layne" which got to No. 20, then "See Emily Play" that did better getting to No. 3, both in 1967. By '68 Syd, through a combination of mental health issues and too many drugs, was out of the band and Dave came in. From that moment Floyd could not write a single to save their life. The last UK single until "Brick" was "Point Me at the Sky", which sunk without trace in 1968. They did, however, do the odd promising album, which they will still be playing on the Earth and the Moon in a hundred years' time.

The Dark Side of the Moon from 1973 is one of the biggest selling albums of all time. It is a prog rock classic, full of dark, meaningful lyrics, soaring guitar solos, spoken words snippets and soulful female backing vocals. I loved it, about 30 years later, when I could finally grasp the "old before his time" obtuse Roger Waters lyrics. Two more mega selling albums were to follow. Wish You Were Here and Animals, with lyrics, sentiment and style in a similar vein. Pink Floyd did not do singles.

"Another Brick in the Wall" was taken from multi mega selling 1979 album, The Wall. It was recorded by Roger Waters on bass and vocals, Dave Gilmour on lead guitar and lead vocals, Richard Wright on keyboards and Nick Mason on drums. It was produced by Roger, Dave, James Guthrie and Bob Ezrin. It was the latter that really turned it into a hit. It was Bob who suggested using a local secondary school, Islington Green, to provide a 23-person choir of 13- to 15-year-olds to sing on the verse/chorus in the second half of the song. He had previously put a children's choir on "School's Out" by Alice Cooper as a producer in 1972. The music teacher, Alun Renshaw at Islington Green was very keen to make this happen, which he did, and the choir were duly recorded. The school got £1000, some concert tickets, a copy of the single and that was that for the moment. However, changes in the law meant that by the late '90s the members of the choir could claim royalties and they were eventually traced by royalties expert Peter Rowan and were then able to receive them.

Lyrically it is just a seven-line verse and chorus repeated twice, once with Dave and Roger singing and secondly with the choir. The words are a diatribe against nasty teachers often found at boarding schools. These are typically angry lyrics from Roger, but they struck a chord with a lot of people. What a contrast with the St. Winifred's School Choir's "Grandma" song the following year! It was still school children, a little younger, but with a song sentiment a million miles away from the

Islington Green choir. It is a complement to our wonderful mixed up pop charts that both singles could get to No. 1 within a year of each other. After the twice repeat of the lyrics, a typical fluid floating Dave Gilmour guitar solo plays out the track.

I was very surprised in 1979 when Floyd released a single. I had followed them in the '70s, having a treasured copy of The Dark Side of the Moon. I did like "Brick" and looking back, I am amazed by its simplicity, just two verses and chorus and one guitar solo, all set to a very simplistic four beats to the bar. Floyd were also famous for not doing dancey tracks and here they were going disco, whatever next? But it worked. Like many of our No. 1s, you could sing along, tap your feet and play air guitar, if you wished. In those punk times of '79, the anti-authority lyrics would have been attractive to promote the spirit of teenage rebellion. In the early '80s I did start my own career as a teacher and I very smugly thought Roger Waters was not talking about me with his anti-teacher lyrics, I was a nice teacher, honest! This was another obvious No. 1 with all the attributes great singles have, almost created accidentally on purpose, because of the vision of producer Bob Ezrin.

It is not a rumour that Pink Floyd, to the best of my knowledge never released another single. They were nearly one hit wonders, a "shoddy" effort from such as wonderful band but then of course, zillions of albums sales later, they had planned it that way. Pink Floyd did not do singles!

Chapter 45

1967: A Whiter Shade of Pale: Procol Harum

Released 12 May 1967
No. 1 for 6 weeks
8 June to 12 July '67
Sales UK: 500,000

It is always a bit sad perhaps, when a band gets its creative peak within a few months of forming and then is still performing 45 years later with just the one big hit. This is a little unfair on Procol Harum, who obtained a good living through their music that was predominantly album orientated over many years. Having said that, they will go down in musical and cultural history as the band that put out "A Whiter Shade of Pale", a single that is rightly considered to be one of the greatest of all time.

Procol Harum were formed in Southend in early 1967 and were named after a cat belonging to a friend of the band. Gary Brooker, the main writer, and singer over the years came up initially with music for "Pale". He could have been listening to "Air on a G String" by J S Bach or Percy Sledge's "When a Man Loves a Woman", or maybe he had taken note of both. These two bits of music can be found lingering in the background of "Pale" as musical influences. Gary wrote on piano but needed an organ to swell out his idea, which Matthew Fisher provided, giving embellishment and elaboration on the Hammond Organ. This organ sound became very much a part of "Pale", yet Matthew did not get a writing credit at the time. Over the years, this has caused some rancour between Gary, who was very protective of "his" song and Matthew, especially as the royalties accrued for 10m copies over the years was rather a lot of money The case went before the Law Lords in 2009 and Matthew won and is now joint musical writer for "Pale" with Gary.

The lyrics cannot be dismissed in a few sentences. They are probably the most enigmatic of all lyrics of all our No. 1 singles, apart from maybe those to "Bohemian Rhapsody" in Chapter 12. Interestingly they both reference the word "Fandango", which is a lively triple meter partner dance found in Spain and Portugal. The moral is, if you want to write some of the greatest songs of all time, it is a good idea to put "Fandango" in the lyrics. Right, time for some analysis and I could get this wrong. Keith Reid wrote the lyrics, and the title is easy enough. He saw someone at a party, who was obviously a bit worse for wear, being described as looking like "a whiter shade of pale" so there was the title. Then it gets tricky, the best I can do is that the lyrics are some sort of decadent psychedelic seduction with Chaucerian references like "the Miller's tale" thrown in to confuse us, and probably Keith himself, even more. All in all, the lyrics are very clearly well sung by Gary, and I like the air of mystery about them. In our book of pop No. 1s obscure, weirder lyrics are quite rare. It is just as well the book is not about prog rock songs, otherwise lyrical analysis could take years.

"Pale" was played by Gary Brooker on vocals and piano, Mathew Fisher on the Hammond Organ, Ray Royer on guitar, David Knights on bass and Bill Eyden on drums. It came out in May '67, subsequently spending six weeks over the summer at No. 1. It was a musical alternative to the Beatles' Sergeant Pepper album that more or less came out at the same time and was No. 1 in the album charts. Both Procol's single and Beatles' album were able to transcend mere music and become part of the cultural landscape of the 1967 summer of love. John Lennon in particular has been quoted as saying that "Pale" was one of his all-time favourite songs. It got to No. 1 in eleven countries in total. It had an amazing accolade of being the most played UK single in public spaces ever up to 2009. It has been used and referenced in numerous films and TV shows over the years. It always features high up in polls of people's all-time favourite songs. Since it came out up to the present day in 2024, it has sold over 10m copies.

Procol Harum continued their musical journey after "Pale". They had a hit with "Homburg" in late '67 and that was it for singles, but they had a worthy career as prog, art rock titans right up to 2022 when Gary Broker aged 77 passed away. They finally broke up after that.

My own view is that this is a great song, one of the best, if not the best. The song is timeless. It could be released in any era and would still be a hit. There are up to 1000 cover versions of "Pale", one of the best from the '90s, being by Annie Lennox. The original with "contributions" from J S Bach, Percy Sledge, Matthew Fisher, Keith Reid and Gary Brooker is the best. This is a great example of a song that is somehow more than the sum of its parts. It is that good, that I think of it as a song that escaped from heaven and luckily landed on Procol Harum's lap. Not a bad way to finish up our 45 No. 1s perhaps, with saving the very, very best until last.

A Book End: Outro

As I have gone through the 45 No. 1 singles, I have gone out of my way to not say whether a song could be described as "good, bad or ugly". It is quite obvious what my view of a song is, and I would like to re-emphasise that I picked singles that were diverse to show how mixed up the charts were over the span of TOTP from 1964 to 2006. The songs included pure pop, pop rock, easy listening, dance pop, novelty comedy, charity and just the one instrumental, which lent itself to the title of this book. I wanted to get as big a range as possible to represent all the charts could offer, as No. 1s, over the years. They are not the best singles of all time or even the best single for each year of TOTP. But we have to remind ourselves that they all got to No. 1 and for that week(s), they were officially the best and most popular song on offer at that time.

It is fitting to pay tribute to the many singers, artists, songwriters, bands, producers, engineers, and even support people who just made the tea, for all the creativity, hard work, and in some cases the absolute cheek, in persisting to make their song the very best it could be. You also have to give credit to artists who put out some wonderfully weird efforts that could not possibly get to No. 1, could they? They did of course; thanks to the risks that were taken and for that they deserve our eternal thanks. These songs have given joy, pleasure and emotional support to millions and have been the soundtrack of our lives. Some of the artists have passed away or are elderly and infirm, being unable to perform anymore but their music lives on in records, videos and most importantly in our collective memories, never to be forgotten.

It is of interest to compare my soon to be revealed chart rundown with the UK sales figures for the 45 singles. These figures are included in the rundown list coming up on the right by each single. However, as indicated in the Intro, because of the difficulty of finding exact number of sales, these figures have been rounded up and are sometimes approximations. In the case of Mr Blobby his sales figures are, of course, a downright exaggeration (Er…only joking Blobster!). There are sixteen of the 45 songs that got 1m sales or more, including six of them in my top 10. My list of my top 10 favourites does include the top three selling singles from the 45, which are "Bohemian Rhapsody" with 2.6m, Do They Know It's Christmas?" with 3m and "Candle in the Wind '97" with 5m. However, my favourite, soon to be announced, is not one of the biggest sellers, being well below a million. "Crazy in Love" by Beyoncé, a 2.4 m seller was only able get to No. ? in my rundown (I am not telling, will keep you in suspense for another paragraph). Both these songs are outliers to the general trend. Now if I was crazy enough to do a scatter graph you might just see some sort of correlation or relationship between single sales and my own chart rundown, the more sales the higher, to some extent, my chart placing for the chosen singles. I think, generally speaking, there are songs in the list that have a universal appeal to all, sell well and even me, strange man that I am, like and have them appropriately high in my chart. In general, the higher the song in my chart, then the greater its UK sales.

Right, that's the maths lesson over. Now it is time for the controversial yet fun part, where you might totally disagree with my chart rundown choice of our 45 songs. There is no refund available and if you do not like my choice, you could always do your own list to amusingly irritate your friends and family if you wish. In a spirit of wilful, blatant, self-opinionated subjectivity, I will go down the list of my least to most favourite song as a "singles chart" from 45 to 1. This is not entirely dependent on record sales as I have indicated above, cultural significance, or what the critics said. It is my choice only. This should, I hope, create much debate, disagreement and be a major talking point for readers, fans and nerdy listy types alike. I suspect most people would perhaps broadly agree with my rundown but perhaps not for the specific place for a specific song. No one might expect "Mr Blobby" to get to No. 1 or "Bohemian Rhapsody" to only sneak in at 45, but then again you never know?

Right here goes. Coming in at No 45 is... You do know, you've guessed it!

45.	Mr Blobby	Mr Blobby	600,000
44.	There's No One Quite Like Grandma	St. Winifred's School Choir	1m
43.	The Chicken Song	Spitting Image	200,000
42.	Release Me	Engelbert Humperdinck	1.38m
41.	Mambo No. 5	Bob the Builder	400,000

Bubbling under at No 40 is...

40.	Back Home	England World Cup Squad	250,000
39.	Deeply Dippy	Right Said Fred	200,000
38.	Grandad	Clive Dunn	772,000
37.	Billy Don't Be a Hero	Paper Lace	200,000 approx.
36.	Come On Eileen	Dexys Midnight Runners	1.33m

Zooming in at No. 35 is...

35.	Millennium	Robbie Williams	400,000
34.	The Combine Harvester (Brand New Key)	The Wurzels	250,000

33. Je T'aime… Moi Non Plus	Jane Birkin and Serge Gainsbourg	250,000
32. A Little Less Conversation	Elvis vs JXL	800,000
31. Crazy in Love	Beyoncé	2.4m

Carrying on down with No. 30 is…

30. Spinning Around	Kylie Minogue	400,000
29. (Is This the Way to) Amarillo	Tony Christie with Peter Kay	1.2m
28. He Ain't Heavy, He's My Brother	The Hollies	500,000
27. Ride on Time	Black Box	1.1m
26. Wannabe	Spice Girls	1.38m

Dancing down the motorway to No. 25 is…

25. Livin' la Vida Loca	Ricky Martin	352,000
24. The Good, the Bad and the Ugly	Hugo Montenegro	200,000 approx.
23. Tainted Love	Soft Cell	1.05m
22. Billie Jean	Michael Jackson	500,000
21. Call on Me	Eric Prydz	300,000

Warbling along under the oak tree with No. 20 is…

20. Some Might Say	Oasis	458,000
19. Hips Don't Lie	Shakira with Wyclef Jean	1m
18. Telegram Sam	T. Rex	200,000 approx.
17. (Everything I Do), I Do It for You	Bryan Adams	1.87m
16. Vogue	Madonna	663,000

Singing down the highway with No. 15 is…

15. Knowing Me, Knowing You	ABBA	976,000
14. 19	Paul Hardcastle	785,000
13. It's a Sin	Pet Shop Boys	500,000
12. Wuthering Heights	Kate Bush	600,000
11. Cum On Feel the Noize	Slade	500,000

And bursting into the top 10 with…

10. Video Killed the Radio Star	Buggles	600,000
9. Love Is All Around	Wet Wet Wet	1.91m
8. I Want to Hold Your Hand	The Beatles	1.8m
7. Do They Know It's Christmas?	Band Aid	3m

| 6. | Candle in the Wind '97 | Elton John | 5m |

Now filtering down to the terribly terrific top 5 with…

| 5. | Another Brick in the Wall | Pink Floyd | 1m |
| 4. | (I Can't Get No) Satisfaction | The Rolling Stones | 600,000 |

These top 3 are very much interchangeable. They are probably three of the best singles of all time, recognised by the critics and the general public. For me, they are the best songs of my 45 45s and before I decide the final order, I will take an hour off for a deep ponder… Right, that's done. In the top 3 are…

3.	Bohemian Rhapsody	Queen	2.6m
2.	Good Vibrations	The Beach Boys	600,000
1.	A Whiter Shade of Pale	Procol Harum	500,000

So "A Whiter Shade of Pale" is my winner, with "Good Vibrations" second. I suspect the nation would probably go for "Bohemian Rhapsody". There is nothing in it really, all three were very close. I had to make a choice and "A Whiter Shade of Pale" just "shaded" it to the top in "my book"!

That is that. How to finish this book? How about this:

You have been reading "The Good, the Bad and the Ugly: The Story of 45 Mixed Up No. 1 Songs" with me, the author Richard Taylor. I will see you next time, with my new book called "More Good, Bad and the Ugly: 45 Slightly Less Mixed Up No. 1s"… (perhaps?)

Bye for now.

Bibliography

The main reference book I used was:

The Guinness World Records Book of British Hit Singles & Albums 2005.

As I only went up to 2006, this book was more than adequate in providing basic chart information for nearly all the songs over the years. Otherwise, I used the internet for referencing numerous artist websites sites, in addition to three more specific ones.

Officialcharts.com
Songmeanings.com
Songfacts.com

I also might have had a sneaky peek every now and again at:

Wikipedia!

But that is our little secret.